A Centaur Speaks

A New and Exciting Way to Integrate Your Psyche

By Eric Barkemeyer

A Centaur Speaks
A New and Exciting Way to Integrate Your Psyche

By Eric Barkemeyer

Other Books by the Author

In the Wink of an Angel's Eye

ACKNOWLEDGMENTS

I would like to thank Sue Ray for her invaluable time, patience, critical assessment, ideas, and technical assistance in helping me create this book.

I would like to thank Chris Rasmussen for her assistance and contribution in helping develop some of the early ideas of the horse/rider theory.

Table of Contents

INTRODUCTION

Accepting mutually incompatible
Viewpoints gracefully

This book, at its best, is meant to be interactive. It is about you. I am merely your guide and humble servant. I want you to undertake a daring quest, a journey to explore your inner self, to find out who you Really are. This adventure will be fun and scary but it is worth it, as an unfathomably rich treasure patiently awaits you. A treasure you have been relentlessly searching for your whole life. I want you to Really explore yourself in a unique and curious way.

For this quest we will require a trusty steed, a horse with great power and full of passion. And we will need a rider for him with great determination and knowledge. Together they are fearless and unbeatable. Separate, they are a pale shadow of the totality. They will both need all of their strength and cunning if they are to confront the mighty Centaur. Only together will they be able to decipher a treasure map. You start with a treasure map that is in the disguised form of a series of questions, as an immature wizard transformed it long ago. He did not want the secrets revealed. The questions will give you a feel for your character that will start the journey. And after your adventure is over, if you are fearless enough to find the deeply buried treasure, you will have found that your answers to the questions have mysteriously changed. The greatest adventure ever devised is the one you are living right now. Good luck and may the Centaur be with you.

In the following set of questions, check off what best describes you. And to be of any value you must be brave enough to answer honestly.

If you had to pick one, which of the following represents you MORE than the other?

Science	___	Art	___
Individual activities	___	Group activities	___
Functionality	___	Aesthetics	___
Predictable	___	Unpredictable	___
Efficient, Orderly	___	Not a priority	___
Self-Control	___	Self expression	___
Saving money	___	Spending money	___
By the Book	___	Interpretive	___
Structured	___	Unstructured	___
Responsible	___	Carefree	___
Details	___	Concepts	___
Serious	___	Playful	___
Being in charge	___	Not being in charge	___
Being precise	___	Not a priority	___
Planning ahead	___	Spontaneity	___
Likes numbers	___	Doesn't like numbers	___

Now we can discover something interesting about you, the reader. The left side of the choices all illustrate ideals of the knowledgeable "rider" and the right side of the choices all illustrate ideals of the passionate "horse". There were a total of 16 questions. Count up the number of checks on the left side (rider) and then the number of checks on the right side (horse) in order to find your secret number. For only those adept in the arcane skill of mathematics dare proceed. If your score was between 16/0 and 12/4 then you are a Type 1 character. If your score was between 11/5 and 8/8 then you are a Type 2 character. If your score was between 8/8 and 5/11 then you are a Type 3 character. If your score was between 4/12 and 16/0 then you are a Type 4 character. Now that you know your Type, we can fit you for your armor. Let's delve deeper into a much more important part of your character. What Level of Integration are you? This will help determine what weapons you can carry on your quest.

Go back to the questionnaire and take it again, but this time but a check next to the pairs that you could have checked either way. The ones you were sitting on a fence about, not the ones that were black and white, easy choices. If you had 0 to 4 checked you are slightly Integrated. If you had 5 to 8 checked, you are a Level 1 Integration. If you had 9 to 12 checked you are a Level 2 Integration. And if you had 13 to 16 checked, you are a Centaur.

So far, this adventure has begun with many questions, as adventures often do. What does all this mean to you, as far as what challenges you will encounter in your adventure and how successfully you deal with those challenges? The answers you gave will determine how successful you are currently in your business and personal relationships. And after reading this book, you will be able to dramatically increase how successfully you deal with both. In order to accomplish this, I first have to ask you to bear with me as I have to explain some things, like, what the four Types are all about, what they signify, what an Integration is, what it signifies, and what the heck a mythological creature like a Centaur has to do with it all. Before the Adventure unfolds, let's find out more about the character who dares to challenge the wizard.

Have you ever been at odds with yourself? Have you ever felt like your own worst enemy? Have you ever felt like you have shot yourself in your own foot? Who hasn't? Many of us remember incidents where we did things that were not in our best interests and sometimes quite the opposite. Be it:

-not listening enough to your fears,...**OR**
-being at the mercy of your fears

-not taking time to smell the flowers
(too much discipline), ... **OR**
-procrastinating (lack of discipline)

-not reacting to this or that,... **OR**
-over reacting to this or that

-should I fight it,... **OR**
-should I accept it.

Which of the preceding pairs of choices would you choose to best describe how you live your life, the former or latter? Would you like to be able to change any of your answers? Your answers will tell you a lot about yourself and what this adventure is all about, because prior to setting out on a grand quest, we must first be properly prepared if we truly wish to be successful. The most important preparation for such an undertaking is knowing your true character. We often run into all sorts of opposing situations where we are at odds with our character. The point of the preceding pairs of apparently conflicting desires (as well as the preceding questionnaire) isn't so much the problems themselves, which are instructive, but rather, more importantly, the divisiveness between the radically opposing ideas. Notice how sharply the first part of the pairs differs from the second. How often it seems to be one choice Or the other and how seldom it seems to be both. I suggest a different approach which will permit a lot more success in business, personal relationships and any other area of life you wish to apply it to. Expand your And.

Often it is too much of this, or too much of that, which leads to too little of this and too little of that. Thus, we usually end up with either too much feeling (horse in charge) or too much thinking (rider in charge) about the problem. We are not often at the balance point, like a seesaw teetering between the two extremes and rushing right through the point of balance or harmony. Spending time at the extremes takes energy to get there and energy to go back. How about exploring the peace and energy that comes from the balance point instead of the exhausting swings that are usually filled with tension that produce conflict.

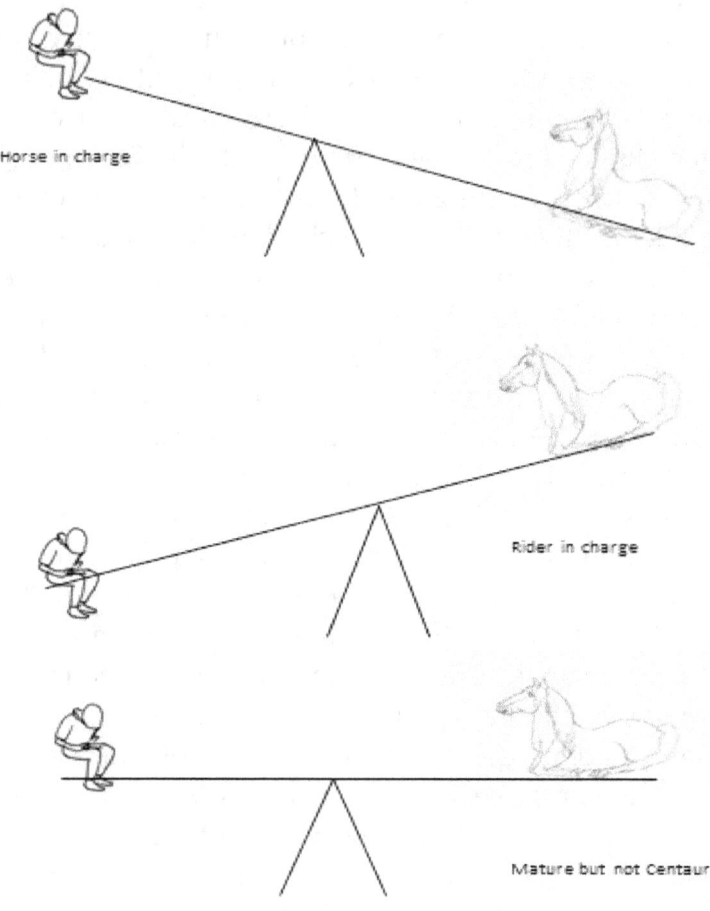

Horse in charge

Rider in charge

Mature but not Centaur

Usually, the seesaw teeters between the realms of thinking or feeling. We obviously use both in our daily lives but we do have a preference or orientation. Which way you lean will be manifested in your personality traits. People who emphasize feelings can be more emotionally reactive for better or worse. People who emphasize thinking can be more analytical for better or worse. But most of our time seems to be spent teetering. Why isn't the middle ground the most common state? The "And" instead of the "Or". This constant imbalance creates tension in everything we do.

The type of person we are determines how far it teeters away from the balance point and how we react to the change. What type of person are you?

There are two parts to the Introduction in this book. The first part speaks to the "horse" side of people. The second part speaks to the "rider" of people. Some people will relate to one and some to the other. My quest is to relate to both of them And to get them to relate to each other.

Getting back to the questionnaire in the beginning, if you said yes to the first part of those questions you probably have difficulty relating to people who answered yes to the second part of those questions. Notice how all of the first choices are related. Notice how all of the second choices are related. There is a very important reason for this and it determines how you live your life and the cause of many problems in your life and how you deal with them.

For most of the people who answer these questions, the answers generally do not overlap. That is, it is not common to honestly say yes to the first and second parts of the questions. There is a definite difference because one is representing one side of the seesaw versus the other. And many conflicts result between people who check off a lot more of one side versus the other. What would it be like to check off all the choices? Why isn't it like this? Is it even possible? Would it help in our personal or business relationships? Would we be more successful in life?

Everyone wants to understand what kind of person they are so they can feel more in harmony with themselves. This would also vastly help in our personal relationships.

In one of life's adventures we are tossed on a stormy, wind-swept ocean in a small raft with self-inflicted holes in it. We try to bring other people into our struggling raft but this only causes the raft to sink faster and we curse the tumultuous storm. We need to fix the raft first before we try bringing others in. This involves understanding the nature of the holes in your raft and what caused them. But we all possess the ability to not only patch the holes but we can also help calm the stormy sea itself, so it is easier to repair the holes. This will make our relationships more successful. People looking for a loving relationship often are said to be looking for the right person. Well, how about first making yourself the "right" person? This involves knowing who we really are.

We all want to know who we really are so we can find our balance point. Where is your balance point? Who are you, really? Most people sense it is a vital learning experience to figure out who we really are. We all think we know who we are but we are never right. We are constantly evolving and we are constantly amazed that there is always more to us than we thought. We also look at the universe thru filters or masks that cloud results. The immature wizard has caste his foggy spell.

To truly understand who we are, you have to be (A) willing to learn and (B) be able to learn and (C) have the knowledge to learn. The fact you are reading this book demonstrates you have achieved A and B. Hopefully this book is the C that lets you proceed further with A and B. This will assist you in resolving and understanding the conflicts with in us all.

I personally observed a demonstration of this these ideas when I was leading a group of people on a challenging horse ride paralleling a very steep slope. There was a steep drop-off down slope and a steep rise up slope. I told them all when you get to the steep part don't pull your horse's reins up the hill slope, but rather give the horse his head (trust him) and you will be fine. Very few people did this. Instead they pulled the horse's head up the hill slope to control his direction, believing that the horse might commit suicide by going off the other side if they didn't pull him up the slope. The odd part about it, is that the horse tends to fight the bit by pulling the other way, down the hill slope, which makes the rider pull harder up slope. The whinnying of the horse after it is yanked on actually makes the rider more scared so he pulls even harder.

Both are fighting and getting frustrated with the other, making it possible to cause an accident (sometimes the horse would actually go up the hill slope which is equally as dangerous and scary). But riders don't generally trust the unpredictable horse (you never know what they might do), believing the horse might kill them. And the horse thinks the rider is causing the problem (the horse has done this ride hundreds of time before with no problem, just trust him) and the rider might kill him. I ask the reader which side of the hill slope debate they empathize with, the horse or the rider? It demonstrates what kind of person you are and that determines how you deal with the universe and the people in it.

So, there is a conflict between horse and rider where each thinks it knows best and there is a lot of wasted energy as they antagonize each other in a fight for dominance, not to mention other possible dangerous side effects. They are essentially adversaries of each other, each right and wrong, each with its own pros and cons. The horse with its perspective is apples and oranges to the rider's perspective, similar to the previously mentioned notion of this "or" that, compared to this "and" that. After witnessing events like these over and over, the idea occurred to me that we each have a horse and rider, metaphorically speaking, inside each of us that causes us to be at odds with our selves. Something every one of us runs into many times each day. I developed a model to show this. Let's use this model to learn more about the nature of the main character in this drama.

The model introduced here is based on previous explored ideas in psychology but I take a new slant on it which explores the interactions between the component parts of the psyche in a different way in order to better integrate our conflicting components. A horse is used to symbolize the feelings and emotions of the psyche. Everything associated with it is elemental, chaotic, reactive, and untamed in the immature state. All of these components give rise to emotions that give rise to feelings that give rise to moods that give rise to personality traits that give rise to "us". Personality traits like emotional reactivity, being impulsive, as well as the other side; love, passion, patience and desire all originate from the horse.

The functions of the body are separate from the horse but it is often through those reactions that we become aware of emotions. Thus the horse and body sometime seem very closely related. And thus sometimes their dividing line is confused. They both have a very different perspective than the rider. But all three have to learn how to get along.

Part of the body consists of instincts, energies, impulses, and biological imperatives, while another part deals with psychological wants, feelings and emotions. Imagine the body component as a 3 year old, which has little or no capacity for delayed gratification. It is primitive and it always wants more right now (the third word a baby generally learns, after mommy and daddy, is "more".) It has no concept of time or rationality. It is the animal within us. It is the basis for what drives us with a burning raw passion. It is a remnant of our evolutionary past prior to civilization. Its needs are physical and sensual, pure organism.

Biologically, it is driven by the limbic system (the most primitive part of the brain). It is the primitive part of the soul we try to safely seal off from the rest of the world. There is only self here and no sense of other. Its perspective is focused outward. There is no self-reflection, nothing is thought out, since there is no reason and no sense of time, only the now. It is propelled by raw, primitive forces with little self-restraint or patience. It only wants its wishes fulfilled now. Humans have felt its power and influence for millions of years and have been dealing with it in all of its "glory" since then.

The immature horse, to date, is often considered tied to the previously mentioned attributes and when the horse surfaces its primitive head, when its desires are not fulfilled, it is said to produce anxiety, depression, phobias, irrational fears, anger etc. The horse is often accused and pronounced guilty of being responsible for producing these pathological elements due to its fundamental nature of reactivity. I view anger, as well as those other mental illnesses, as a sign of an emotionally ill horse. These illnesses are a sincere demand for assistance, like shock is a plea to the physical body to seek a doctor when the body is injured. Similarly, I view fear as a sincere demand from the body for assistance. And the usual solution is to medicate the horse with anti-depressants or ignore its needs altogether. But drugs aren't the only way to make the horse less reactive. It can be calmed by using techniques mentioned in this book. Yes, this book is bad news for the pharmaceutical companies.

The immature horse is often thought of as brutal, reactive, savage, and beast-like, thus an unwanted ally to fight the universe. However, the model introduced here paints a different picture of our dark side. It is only a hairy beast when it is poked and prodded. This state is unnatural and pathological, so it only appears hairy but it usually manifests in this incarnation because it is poked so much.

But instead of the hairy beast, it can be matured and taught to act more like a domesticated horse, possessing elements of train-ability and a willingness to comply which can transform him into a formidable ally. Its interest lies within the unity of the herd. It seeks unity and to be connected with it all. It seeks to comply. It wants to serve and help. Horses can also be reactive but its reactivity can be dampened. It is not totally unreasonable if the proper language is used to communicate with it, like a horse whisperer. It can learn and mature. More importantly, it will become calm and less fearful if one acknowledges its existence and learns its language and the rider stops doing things that agitate it. Then the body becomes calmer and healthier as well.

The central theme here is that the rider is a primary cause of the problems. If one does not abuse and exploit the horse by driving it into the ground but instead allow it the rest it needs, and address its injuries, then the horse becomes calmer, less fearful and thus easier to manage. The principle is that the optimum state of the horse is one of calmness or peace, just as we are considered healthy in the absence of disease or injury. Thus calming the rider calms the horse which calms the body. Then there is peace. Incessant thoughts cease.

The rider's function is to harness the horse through discipline, knowledge, and reason. Its perspective is focused inward. It is the entity that controls the spurs and the reins of the horse. In our society the rider is taught to exploit the horse the same way we exploit the earth, no coincidence. It is the mechanism to focus and manage the power and energy of the horse and to use its abilities in an attempt to predict the future through the use of knowledge which gives a sense of control. It developed rules to control the horse. It assists in problem solving and it also developed language to communicate its ideas. The rider seeks to mitigate and satisfy the sources of the internal tension produced by the horse's energy in an efficient manner but often this ends up just agitating the horse.

The rider can sometimes be thought of as a small, scared and terrified passenger desperately trying to control the wild beast any way it can. Alternatively, it sometimes can manifest as a gigantic gorilla beating the smaller, helpless horse with a stick till it complies. It all depends on which way the seesaw currently teeters.

But the rider depends on the horse to manifest reality, for landing a job, finding a mate, gathering resources. The rider is dependent on this powerful force contained within the horse that is, at times, compliant and peaceful and other times fractious and even dangerous.

The rider relentlessly searches for patterns in an otherwise baffling world in order to better understand and predict actions of the universe that can either save or threaten its existence. The rider with its rationality is beholden to the horse to make its thoughts a reality and manifest its goals. If the rider is smart and uses its knowledge and understanding skillfully, it can forge an alliance with the horse and the nature of the relationship can change. It can be one of a gentle, calm, relaxing ride through a meadow by a river instead of a rodeo fraught with chaotic, unknown and dangerous outcomes.

The rider is responsible for the rise of civilization (about 5,000 years ago) and its associated rules, laws, and conventions. Though, biologically, the pre-frontal cortex (the last part of the brain to evolve, the rider part) has been around much longer. Its rapid ascension to its current dictatorial status has been something we have been dealing with it in all its "glory" since then. The rider's traditional approach to the horse is usually to tighten its grip to maintain control. But the more it tightens its grip the more the horse will "slip through its fingers", so to speak.

The horse and rider are two of the prime characters in this adventure. They can be allies or adversaries which assist or impede you in your quest. We learned about their attributes way back in the beginning of this journey. Getting back to the questionnaire in the beginning, the left side of the choices all illustrate rider ideals and the right side of the choices all illustrate horse ideals.

Now, everybody has elements of both horse and rider within themselves but one is usually preferred over another. There is a general orientation or preference manifested through one's personality traits. The chart below lists typical horse and rider personality traits. It also shows there are mature and immature versions of the horse and rider which correspond to strengths and weaknesses. I use the word immature a lot in this book but I do not assign the negativity that usually goes along with it. Immaturity, to me, means just undeveloped.

	Rider	**Horse**
MATURE	Not fearful Stable Dependable Achievements Disciplined Structured Organized Reserved Reliable Cautious	Not fearful Spontaneous Carefree Laissez Faire Calm Fun loving Patient Easy Going Sensory- Oriented Nurturing
IMMATURE	Fearful Angers Easily Controlling Highly Critical Unyielding No Apologies Judgmental Stubborn Demanding	Fearful Irresponsible Impulsive Unreliable Disorganized Reactive Gullible

You probably know people who typically exemplify these traits. The rider orientated people are the more achievement orientated, courageous, analytical, academically orientated, but also, when immature, never apologize, are strict, "my way or the highway", controlling, type persona.

There are strengths and weakness in each of the horse and rider perspectives depending on their strength or maturity. The more infighting between horse and rider, the less productive and energetic they are, and thus more of the immature traits tend to surface. Immature traits manifest more depending on which wins and the cost of the battle. More energy tends to make us stronger. Many times the battle reduces the strength of each. Which traits would you prefer to manifest in yourself to battle against the daunting universe?

The rider perspective is focused inward and on the future, so they interpret the universe in terms of their self. When a rider isn't doing anything he is still constantly thinking. Thinking and thoughts are constant companions even when walking through a peaceful, beautiful meadow.

The horse orientated persona is honest, a people-pleaser, unstructured, has a good sense of humor but also, when immature, emotionally reactive and fearful. Their perspective is focused outwards and on the "now" so they interpret the universe as occurring outside of self. The horse perspective manifests as feelings constantly running through its head. Feelings are constant companions when walking through a peaceful, beautiful meadow.

You may have noticed that there is a correlation between the rider personality traits and those of a stereotypical male. And you may have noticed there is a correlation between the horse personality traits and those of a stereotypical female. I leave it to the reader to decide if these opposite perspectives produce the divisiveness that explains the 50%

divorce rate, and the notion that men are from Mars and women are from Venus.

So, there is the horse and rider fighting to see which will lead in life, each with its own different, but valuable perspective. Is this all there is to it? No.

There is also another entity that influences the horse and rider system. That is, the Universe, the stuff outside ourselves. By "the Universe" I mean all the trials and tribulations found in life; the problems, angst, needs, frustrations and challenges that confront us in our daily lives.

The interaction between the horse, rider and universe manifests itself in a type of chain of command. The powerful universe sends a challenge that the rider attempts to solve or deal with by using its knowledge and discipline, the emotions and feelings of the horse, and the energy of the body. Sometimes the rider has to resort to muti-tasking to achieve results when the universe throws multiple tasks at it. This forces it to draw more from the horse who draws more from the body which has a limit. The rider develops techniques which allow it to multi-task but the horse doesn't prefer to multi-task and also has a limited supply of energy to divide among all these demands. Sometimes the body doesn't have the energy for all these requests and the system breaks down. A lot of people live their lives near this limit of the body's energy. They also don't give the horse a chance to recharge or heal from the exertions and the horse has nowhere to turn to get more energy. This, in turn, upsets the horse because it can't help anymore.

So when the universe gives us a problem, the rider uses knowledge to solve it or the rider develops an adaptation to deal with it. If this doesn't work he uses the horse's abilities to assist with it. When the horse and body are nearly exhausted, and the problem still can't be dealt with, then the problem should be avoided. If the problem can't be avoided, there is a total break-down of the system and illness results as the body is last in line in this chain of command. The total break-down of the body is the end of the line but the problem will get solved somewhere along this line, one way or another.

The quest is to deal with it before it gets this bad, so we don't have to wield a lot of heavy armor all the time. But operating any system continually at or near the breaking point is not productive, though humans are excellent at living in toxic environments, unfortunately. The best systems have reserves built in to deal with the inevitable times when the system is tasked, but keeping the system charged from the beginning is the best procedure. We have to learn to use our available energy supply more productively without wasting it in needless internal battles that reduce the strength of horse and rider.

So far I have mentioned that human behavior can be polarized between two extremely opposing poles exemplified by the horse and rider model. How we respond to the universe's trials and tribulations depends on whether one is horse or rider orientated. But also, how well the horse and rider are integrated and the relative strength of each.

The horse and rider are often opposed to one another as they are apples and oranges to each other.

Some people aren't simply horse or rider orientated but rather, integrated together. There is an evolution as the apple and orange (horse and rider) become like a salad. The individual components are still identifiable (like in a salad) but they are called something different, a "salad". But in this "salad" they are essentially still separate, slightly integrated. Thus they have elements of both but there is still a tension. Instead of truly integrating, they flip back and forth very quickly so it appears to be an integration. It is an awkward integration and for future reference in this book, I will refer to this as a Level 1 Integration.

Upon future evolution it is possible for the Level 1 Integration to become a "soup". Thus, the parts are now homogeneous, the parts are not now separate but one unit. Now there is no tension or conflict because both parts agree, as there is essentially one part. As this "soup" evolves, it becomes more consistent, meaning this behavior becomes the norm, and it evolves to become the "entree". For future reference in this book, I will refer to this "soup" as a Level 2 Integration. And the entree will be referred to as a Level 3 Integration.

To facilitate the understanding of the nuances of this principle, I introduce 4 basic personality types based on an increasing percentage of horse to rider. I describe the rider orientated character as Type 1. Type 2 is a rider oriented character with some horse in them, like the Level 1 Integration. Type 3 is a horse oriented character with some rider in them, again the Level 1 integration. Type 2 and 3's are both a blend of Type's 1 and 4. Type 4 is the horse oriented character.

I will go into more interesting and provocative details about these Types throughout the book and their roles in personal relationships in Chapter 5. But first let's find out more about you.

In order to show, in practical terms, what these Types are like in reality, I take the example found in the earlier quiz of the "saver of money" versus the "spender". The saver of money would be an expression of the Type 1 personality. They believe in saving money and know unequivocally this is the right and best thing to do. No doubts whatsoever. One should save money for the inevitable "rainy day". A type 2 personality would save money but feel the regret of denying themselves the pleasure of spending money, thus showing the blending of horse and rider traits. They would be conflicted. A type 3 personality would spend money but feel guilty about doing it. Thus they also would be conflicted and this again shows the blending of the horse rider traits. A type 4 would spend money and feel no conflict at all. It feels right to do so. No doubts whatsoever.

Curiously, as we will see later, the Type 2 or Type 3 tend to lose in the short run but win in the long run, as the resolution of their conflict allows them to be more diversified than Type 1 or 4, which gives them a broader perspective which will benefit them in the long run. (Type 2 and 3 are the Level 1 Integration). Though in the beginning, the black and white world of the Type 1 and 4 does provide less conflict and appears more stable and simple but at the expense of a broader perspective.

The important point here is that one can take any of the personality traits mentioned previously in the questionnaire, say like I just did with spending money, and apply the same analysis to them regarding the personality types.

I will say here, and it will be explained further again, that the Level 1 integration can further evolve into a Level 2 Integration. Then, at this stage, there is a smooth, seamless, graceful approach to one's horse and rider, and to the universe's trials and tribulations. Finally, when the Level 2 Integration becomes consistent (when one learns to routinely harmonize opposites), and this approach is used almost all the time, then the horse and rider have merged to become similar to the Centaur (a mix of horse and man) of Greek mythology, a Level 3 Integration.

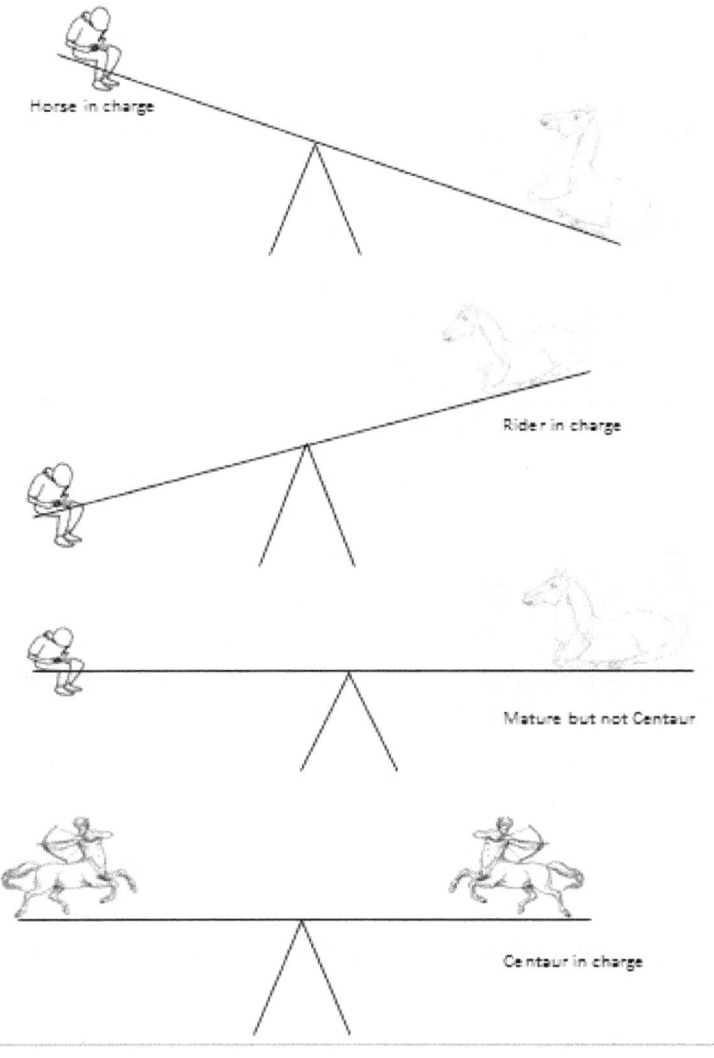

Horse in charge

Rider in charge

Mature but not Centaur

Centaur in charge

I also point out that the emotional pain associated with the transition between these Levels lessens as you evolve through your journey. Also, happiness increases, stress reduces, and it gets easier to integrate as you progress along this path.

As a practical example of how the four Types manifest in everyday life and create problems, and how to avoid them, I illustrate with a real life story.

A rider orientated Type 1 person called "B" was riding in a car with a horse orientated Type 4 person called "J". They were both adults, and sisters as a matter of fact. They were on their way to B's vacation home to clean it. They were about to pick up some of B's rider orientated friends when B said to J, "Now my friends we will be picking up here aren't like you and I need you to act right among them. No wearing skimpy clothes, no criticizing them, no off color comments, no curse words. This is my vacation house we are going to. Just so you know the rules." J acknowledged this at the time and abided by the rules during her stay but after the cleaning of the vacation home was finished, and they had dropped B's friends off, J had time to ruminate (being a horse) on all of this and had something to say to B (naturally in an emotional tone of voice). "That was very offensive, making me conform to who you think I should be. You made me feel like a second class person who has to be told how to act with proper people, like you are embarrassed by me and my "primitive" habits. I am who I am and being my sister you should accept this. I don't tell you how to act and dress. l treat you like an adult and not a child. Why didn't you tell your friends to have some tolerance for people and not be so rigid. Why didn't you ask them to change?"

This is a typical story of a Type 4 horse and Type 1 rider having opposing viewpoints and how it plays out. I do point out that there are mature and immature Types of all 4 kinds and this exchange was an example of immature types. Now I will replay the story but instead of a Type 1 and Type 4 having the discussion, I will use a Type 2 and Type 3 having it. I will use the same names for convenience.

"Now my friends we will be picking up here are a little stuffy and old fashioned in their opinions. I want everybody to be comfortable with everyone so we all need to have some tolerance and patience with our differences. These people can be a little difficult to deal with. It would really help me out if maybe you could dress just a little more conservatively and tone down colorful comments a little. I know they can be uptight and rigid and sometimes I have a hard time dealing with it but I hope you have the patience to deal with them so everybody gets along. I will do my best to help smooth over any rough spots between you. You are my sister and I love you."

J looked at her and grimaced. "I'm miffed that you would think I might not get along with your prissy friends." Silence for a few minutes. "But, I guess you have a point. People can be stuffy like that. I guess I can be a bit much at times because my emotions can get the best of me and I can make some off color remarks. Thanks for understanding. I guess I'll try to do my best to watch what I say and how I dress. I know there are times when I should watch myself a little more closely. Sometimes I wish I had more of your sense of control. I'm working on that. You are my sister, so I will try."

The primary difference between the two stories, and the two outcomes, is the large lack of understanding between the Type 1 and Type 4 in the first story and the higher level of understanding between the Type 2 and Type 3 in the second. I point out again that I chose immature versions of the Type 1 and Type 4 to make a point. However immaturity is rather common among humans. The Type 2's can understand and actually feel how the other Type 3 feels. Type 2's and 3's have a broader perspective so they act accordingly. (I will go into more detail about the four Types in the next chapter.) They demonstrate traits of both so they can understand the other and the other understands them.

Both Type 1 and Type 4 in the first story believe they were "Right" and the other was totally at fault. No doubts. No conflict in themselves but only with the other. Both have a limited perspective. Both also happen to believe that they have an integrated perspective. And if you can agree with that perspective you will get along with them. Both stories also show how all Types can have some valid points.

Often with humans it's not what you say but how you say it. The rider thinks about what is said and the horse feels how it is said. Both horse and rider pick up on this. The second example shows a "Level 1 integration" with a more mature approach. "J" still had her feelings hurt, but realized that her relationship with her sister was the higher priority so agreed to compromise in this situation. "B" still wanted to have her wishes followed, but did respect her sister enough to not disregard her feelings or force her to completely change. An integration of horse and rider occurs here, though awkwardly, but the disagreement was minor and short-lived, as a compromise could be reached. Each one gained something and gave up something to maintain the relationship.

Now when Type 2 and Type 3 can integrate these two components (horse and rider) smoothly and gracefully into a "Level 2 integration" level of maturity, then no disagreement ever would have occurred in the first place because each would intuitively respect, understand and be willing to accept the others position without having to discuss it in advance. In this situation, "B" would have not been concerned with rules or appearances due to the casualness of the event. "J" would respect her sister's role as hostess and watched her behavior in order to be a good guest and respect her sister. Neither would have lost anything or gained anything. Even compromise wouldn't have been required.

The goal of this book is to understand and acknowledge the existence, various roles, and strengths of the horse and rider; to understand the perspectives and goals of each and to learn how to efficiently integrate the two components into a compatible, unified whole with the body. This will allow one to become like the "Centaur" of Greek mythology which was half horse and half human, incorporating elements from each to become more than the sum of the parts. The Centaur realizes if you take care of your horse it will take care of you.

A Centaur truly is free as it has successfully integrated the horse and rider components. It now has a free CHOICE how to act using horse "and" rider ideas at its discretion. It can actually flip the switch back and forth gracefully between the two elements with neither feeling slighted. Thus a

Centaur, if he wants, can smoothly Choose to be a Type 1 today and a Type 4 tomorrow. How often would we like to just flip a switch to gracefully integrate the two elements that would allow us to make the "correct" choice? You might say the Centaur's horse can "think" and the Centaur's rider can "feel". But the Centaur also has a strong horse and rider, having developed both.

The Centaur is also strong enough to resist temptations and not over react to fears. It has a strong sense of gratitude, savors the joys of everyday life, is empathetic, indulges in acts of kindness, has a good social network, copes well, forgives easily, is not distracted easily, and appreciates the simple things in life. It is consistent in its behavior and feelings. It knows what it wants, and what is truly in its best interests and doesn't have one foot out the door in relationships. It doesn't feel "this" way today and "that" way tomorrow. It is mature. Thinking becomes clearer, more focused, and accurate. Feelings become more colorful, powerful, trustworthy and predictable. Love becomes more colorful, powerful and trustworthy and predictable. It can not only love but it can also re-love without regret. Meaning it can take a step back in love and then return. This eliminates baggage.

The Centaur is also non-judgmental, not prone to anger, non-reactive to fears, and realizes that it can be quite productive to let the horse have a romp now and then. The Centaur has outgrown the idea that relaxing the rider will only result in suicide. The result is actually the opposite of suicide.

The Centaur is that elusive quarry possessing the ingenuity to boldly integrate education and entertainment to mesmerize people with its magical, passionate love of life and dazzle people with knowledge of arcane, mysterious, unknown forces that explain the universe. This allows Centaurs to be truly free. They are free from themselves. They can resist temptations and are not controlled by fears. They can be fully trusted. They can love truly. They live in true integrated harmony with themselves and the universe. They have an energy surplus because they don't waste energy on the horse and riding in-fighting. This excess available energy I define as the feeling of "Happiness". Thus, yes, we can all live happily ever-after, for real.

And we can experience Peace from the incessant rider thoughts that can distract us from savoring life. I will also show how the Centaur can expand the individual limits and capabilities of the horse, rider, and the physical body itself, sometimes to extraordinary lengths. This allows your character to more successfully deal with impediments and challenges that the universe cares to throw in your path.

The further goal of this book is to learn that the horse and rider exist, to learn how to use the knowledge to calm both of them, to allow a broader perspective to evolve, to expand your And. And finally to learn how to use the broader perspective to solve most of the problems in your life. A lot of human problems (with ourselves and with the universe) are solvable by becoming a Centaur.

The goal of this book, however, is not to say, "Man I have to go out and buy a horse!"

CHAPTER ONE

There are no such things as opposites,
Only differences, and they don't have
To be opposing.

As I mentioned, the horse and rider can manifest in each person in different ways and degrees. I will now go into details of the 4 personality Types based on the horse-rider model and how they go together. Please keep in mind the four types represent a broad spectrum and do not have black and white (sharp) boundaries. Also keep in mind I make no suggestion that the horse or rider is "better" than the other.

Type 1 is rider orientated. Type 2 is a rider/horse mix with more emphasis on rider than horse. Type 3 is horse /rider with more emphasis on horse than rider. So, basically Type 2 and 3's are simply a blend of the Type 1 and 4's, thus they have some things in common. Type 4 is horse orientated. Most people fall into one Type or another.

It is curious to see if the Type we pick to describe our self is also the same one that others would pick to describe us, as we are not always what others think us to be, or what we think ourselves to be. How accurate your opinion is of your true self reflects your degree of integration. In the preceding story of "B" and "J" I should point out they both believe they are "integrated" people. But neither could step outside their own perspective and neither believed the other could either. The inability to step outside one's perspective is a sign of lack of Integration or immaturity. How does one tell if one is immature? If it bothers you to be called immature, then you are probably immature. And the stronger you react to it, the more immature you are. But if you are immature, it merely means you are fearful. Immaturity is not something to take personally. Nobody wants to be immature. It doesn't help us, quite to the contrary. The important thing is that it can be overcome by strengthening the horse and rider.

Once I have established characteristics of each type I will show how to facilitate relationships between the various types, though this will be done in more detail in Chapter 5. We will see the best way for each type to relate to the other in order to prevent conflicts and conflagrations.

Naturally it can now be seen if a person has integrated their horse and rider (a Level 1 or Level 2 Integration) prior to establishing a relationship it is much easier to have a successful long term relationship. They have learned how to deal with their horse so they now have the tools to deal with another's horse, even if their partner has not yet learned how to do this. Understanding has great benefits, at the very least, it is step 1.

The Type 1 person is rider orientated. Thus they are characterized by being analytical and knowledge based. They have their strengths and weaknesses based on how mature or immature they are.

Strengths include being structured, responsible, stable, consistent, predictable. They are take charge kind of people who are competitive and strong willed.

Weaknesses include being judgmental, overbearing, distant emotionally, highly critical, controlling, quick to anger, opinionated, impatient, stubborn, over bearing, dominating, intolerant of differences. Type 1's would rather be right than happy. In a relationship they offer commitment and reliability. They are independent (but dislike independence in their mate). They don't value emotionality, people out of control of their emotions and they don't put a lot of stock in hope. They tend not to like people who are lazy, unmotivated, or laisse-faire types. In other words they don't get along well with horse type people, or Type 4's.

To deal with this type, you have to relate to them by being factually oriented, pretend you are at a business meeting. They want you to state the facts, be precise and detailed and nothing else, except to tell them what is the benefit to them. In a relationship they want their partner to follow them and their rules and opinions. They don't want non-essential elements talked about. Very rational. They don't like to be questioned, especially with "why" type emotional questions. Things are black and white. If you want to get their attention, tell them how much you appreciate what they do. Appreciation is what drives them. Recognition is valuable to them. They don't like to have their knowledge challenged, as this affects their image. They also value loyalty in a relationship very highly.

Type 2 is the rider/horse orientation with a leaning toward rider. They have a lot of the strengths and weaknesses of the Type 1's but with more of an emotional component. This type of person still emphasizes the mind or knowledge and they are known for being responsible and capable when mature. They enjoy being known for their knowledge and competency and also for their nascent feelings of caring and sympathy. They are independent like the rider and they value deep conversations, honesty, and responsibility.

But they are often conflicted as they have to harmonize the two diverse components of horse and rider. They are the "Level 1 integration" of which I spoke earlier, but they don't know how to smoothly integrate horse and rider yet into all these above traits. They are emotionally distant and emotionally awkward. They spend too much time thinking rather than acting because they feel they have to consult their feelings and this creates conflict. So they appear indecisive, sometimes to the point of self-destruction. They can appear very moody as they try to integrate the horse and rider perspectives. Thus they become skeptical and mistrusting when immature, as they don't know how much value or trust to give to feelings versus rationality. They can thus become high maintenance to deal with, as they constantly flip flop and you never know where you stand with them. They are fearful because the rider and horse don't fully trust each other. They recognize the value of incorporating the horse into decisions but aren't sure exactly whether to trust it. Actually it is also the horse not sure it can trust the rider so they appear conflicted. They become very self-absorbed in order to try to understand how to do this, very inward focused "in their head" types. They value the knowledge of the rider and they value the emotional intuition of the horse but see also the lack in both.

They are like the horse in that they have trouble making commitments, fear the unknown, and are emotionally reactive. The best way to deal with this type is to be a little distant to them. Don't smother them or offer overindulged emotions. Give them all the room you can. Don't push them or they will gallop away.

Type 2's immatures might think, "I shouldn't feel this way", as their rider attempts to control their horse. They might also think, "I must think happy thoughts to cheer myself up", or "Don't think about it if it upsets you". They are self-aware enough to know about emotional self-control but have trouble doing it. It is the rider attempting to force the horse to "think" like a rider.

Level 2 Integrations will do this more smoothly and effortlessly but they have progressed to the point where they accept their horse's moods and don't have a problem with them and thus don't try constantly to question them. A Level 2 Integration can accurately identify what it needs and what it wants and chooses this without conflict and constant reassessing. A Centaur also does this but much more consistently. Each increased level of Integration is easier to achieve and brings with it a deeper degree of happiness, peace and more freedom as the horse / rider conflict reaches resolution.

Type 3 is a horse/ rider mix with the horse dominant but having some rider component. This type of person exhibits strengths which include co - operation and harmony. They like to share things and try hard to make everybody happy. They want to share their emotions more than Type 1's or 2's. They still have the rider traits of valuing stability and confidence but they are emotionally reactive. They have more of the horse's emotions but don't know how to deal with them calmly. They are like the Type 2's in that they are trying to harmonize the horse and rider with in themselves but from more of a horse perspective rather than rider. This is a little harder to do than the Type 2's as the emotional component is stronger and more variable and thus harder to control. They lean toward the emotional and employ intuition when making decisions. So they are more spontaneous but also can become unreliable. They can be emotionally reactive, or explosive and unpredictable with periods of stability. They can go either way, and this makes for unpredictability.

Thus they value stability as a way to help themselves. They have the herd mentality of "we should all stick together". They are good natured but don't like it if this is not appreciated, showing the judgmental nature of the rider. They are thoughtful and caring but not to those they think don't deserve it, again showing the judgmental component of the rider. They value sentimental gestures that show thoughtful consideration. They aren't always sure what they need emotionally except there is a need and it will be expressed.

They are also suspicious of rider's motives. They value the horse sense of caring, sentimentality, generosity, and emotional sensitivity but are suspicious if there is no stability or reliability in them. They, like the Type 2's, need time to deal with harmonizing the two components and don't like to be rushed doing it. They are strong conflict-avoiders which they get from the horse but also like confident take charge types in others which they get from the rider. In dealing with them use patience to give them time to assess both sides of their personality.

The Type 3's are a Level one Integration so they have achieved a level of maturity to achieve this. Once, and if, this type evolves to a Level 2 Integration the strengths become more apparent and the weaknesses and awkwardness disappear resulting in a happier and more successful individual.

Type 4 people are horse orientated. These people value and trust emotion for better or worse. They love to express feelings. They will make a decision because it feels right. They would rather be happy than right.

When immature they can be gullible, naive and fickle and can't ever seem to get anywhere on time, as time is as important to them as it is to a real horse. They aren't very organized and can be sometimes emotionally volatile but not as much as Type 3's because they are more in touch with their emotions.

When mature they appear very well adjusted and happy with themselves and the universe, as the universe is their friend. They are flexible and optimistic. The mature versions are often perceived as the calm one of the bunch or very laid back. Both immature and mature versions share some traits in common. They love to be in a group of people. They dislike controlling, critical, Type 1 people. They trust their emotions. They like to laugh, have a good sense of humor, are spontaneous and go with the flow. They love touching and affection. They are romantics, hopeless romantics. They love to experience it all.

They are idealistic and hate being alone. They love the intimacy of love. To be close to another is the "be and end all". They value freedom and self-expression and always having options. They can make themselves happy where ever they are. When dealing with them always listen and pay close attention. They need lots of reassurance that they are loved. They need a partner that accepts their taking risks, as they appear fearless because they don't always consider consequences, not having a strong rider. They are the most different from everything Type 1. They are as open as the type 1 is closed, for better or worse.

As a practical way to express how these types manifest in real life I use the example of "telling the truth".

A Type 1 would tell the truth when it is when it is in their best interest or on their "agenda". A lie would be acceptable if it furthered their cause and they wouldn't feel bad justifying it if caught.

A Type 2 would "tell the truth" most of the time because it is the "right" thing to do but when caught in a lie would feel bad about it. They might tell a lie to spare feelings (unlike a Type 1) but if caught they would confess and accept consequences.

A Type 3 would tell the truth most of the time because it "feels" right to do so but also uses white lies to spare feelings, but when caught they would feel guilty and confess, even if that might end up making things worse.

A Type 4 would tell the truth most of the time because there is no reason not to. It feels like the right thing to do. When caught in a lie wouldn't feel guilty if it spared another's feelings. That's the most important thing to them.

So, I have described the various types in general but there are other factors which further define them. Maturity and the energy level one is born with are other key components. Maturity will also reflect how energy efficient you are. Immatures tend to not be energy efficient, meaning what energy they have can be utilized in a wasteful and non-productive way. The energy level component is a reflection of the body/horse. Here are some personality traits associated with each type.

Type 1 Immature

Bully Type
Controlling
Physically dominates
Quick to anger
Not cooperative
Abusive
Combative
Intolerant of differences
And if lower energy;
Passive
Geek-like
Difficult to communicate with
Not enthusiastic
Distant emotionally

Type 1 Mature

Leader
Good Physical shape
Productive
Likes Hierarchy
Drive
Focus

If low energy;
Academically oriented
Cautious
Brains behind the CEO

Type 2   Immature

Critical
Emotionally sensitive
Emotionally reactive
Easily distracted
Irresponsible
High maintenance
Conflicted
Self- absorbed
Non- committal
When scared they run
Moody
Gives up easily

Type 2 Mature

Nurturing
Likes deep conversations
Driven
Consistent
Focused
Intuitive
Dependable
Into academics

Type 3 Immature

Emotionally reactive
Unreliable
Scatterbrained
Needy
Passive aggressive
Runs away from conflict
Emotionally explosive
Bad memory
Calm but look out when pushed

Type 3 Mature

Likes harmony
Intuitive
Patient
Sentimental
generous
People pleaser
Into co-operation

Wants everybody happy
Avoids conflict
Loves to give hugs

Type 4 Immature

Emotionally reactive to explosive
Flighty
Disorganized
Doesn't achieve much but always in motion
Loves to play
Not serious about anything
Action without thought
Irresponsible
Overly enthusiastic

If low energy;
Day dreamer
Doesn't accomplish much
Can't focus
Lives in a bubble
Idealistic
Passive
Go with the flow

Type 4 Mature

Unstructured
Care free
Spontaneous
Extroverted
Athletic
Enthusiastic

Loves people gatherings
Focused, productive
Likes the arts

If low energy;
Calm
Easy going
Not much bothers them

I created a diagram to show figuratively how this all goes together.

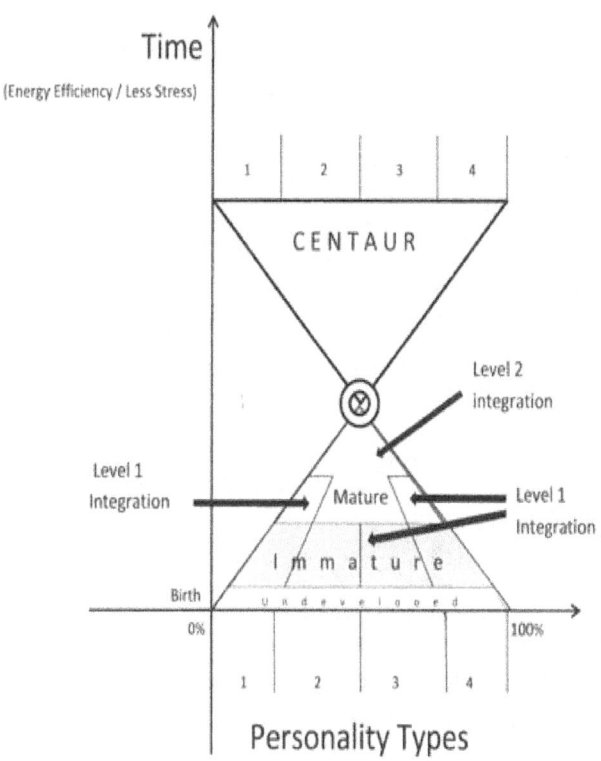

Notice a few interesting things, like the 2's and 3's have different traits at the immature level but become indistinguishable at the mature level because they are closer to becoming Centaurs. They both start out nearer the Centaur when immature as they have traits of both the horse and rider, so they have a shorter distance (hence easier path) to achieve Centaur-hood. 2's and 3's are subsets of 1's and 4's. They are blends. So not having a black and white world of the 1's and 4's, they have to integrate two disparate things and have difficulty doing so, at first.

The immature forms of the Type 2 and 3's have a hard time integrating the two disparate components thus appearing indecisive and not as strong as Type 1 or 4's as they switch rapidly between horse OR rider. They would be often described as wishy-washy. But after maturity they exceed the limitations of the 1's and 4's and become more successful in most pursuits as they have more tools and a broader perspective.

The mature versions just have to fine tune their integration to make the next step to Centaur. The mature versions are learning to become more and more consistent. Also as one integrates, one needs less from the universe so anger becomes displayed less. A Centaur would say, "Once you get angry, you've lost".

The Centaur is consistent. It has developed a new perspective much like what one gets from a near death experience. Things just look different because you realize there are many ways to look at the same thing and the old way isn't the only way to see things. When one becomes a Centaur it is like getting a driver's license. Just because you have one doesn't mean you know how to drive but rather you are given the ability to spend the rest of your life learning to do it better.

The Centaur can truly love as they can be fully trusted as love and trust are integral to each other. Trust comes from consistent behavior and feelings. They don't need something from their mates. They are complete already. They can be respected, another critical component of love.

Now following this idea, it becomes easy to see that a horse OR rider can't always be trusted, because they just can't trust themselves. A Level 1 Integration can be somewhat trustworthy and a Level 2 Integration can be even more trusted, as it is a range. Emotional trustworthiness is a function of how much do you need. The people who need less don't have as many ulterior motives and thus can be trusted more.

Level 2's provide a sound foundation for a relationship as they have the rider to guide and instruct them if the horse gets carried away. The rider is critical for a successful relationship, to control the horse's passion for the subject and pay attention to the logistics of the relationship. I will say the best relationships with the greatest bonds come from people evolving through this process together. Relationships also have to evolve through this process at the same rate. If one is too far ahead of the other, then it drifts off course. When you evolve together through a length of time you can become soul mates, thus one can't be sure their partner is a soul mate until a large period of time has passed. In this process, a person's direction is more important their progress as people sometimes get lost quickly going off course.

But if you find someone who helps you to evolve toward a Centaur hold on to them. We instinctively do this as love is often the result. Love may actually be defined in this way. We instinctively love in some way anyone who helps us to evolve or grow. Unfortunately, in many relationships, not only is there no growth provided, but there is actual retarding of growth as the other person holds us back. This is usually from people who haven't come close to integrating their horse and rider, so they usually are Type 1's or 4's immatures. However I will discuss, in more detail, how the four Types work in personal relationships in Chapter 5.

The Centaur stage means the horse and rider are unified or integrated. They understand each other and thus the Centaur is truly free. The horse and rider are melded as one. There is a true, effortless partnership that both enjoy and respect. The horse trusts the rider and vice versa. Emergent properties then arise that weren't there before integration. True empathy arises. The Centaur is energetic if he/she wishes, or at the very least is most energy efficient. They are not reactive or judgmental. The Centaur makes observations instead of criticisms. They can rise above it all. Anger is rare. They are peaceful, calm, and patient as they can see and truly understand the perspective of all Types. As I said, the Centaur has the Choice of being a Type 1, 2, 3, or 4 whenever they want, whatever is called for. The Centaur will have the strengths of each type, and not be burdened by the weaknesses that sap energy. They have evolved to the point where they can be a partner to any type because of their broader perspective. The civil war between horse and rider is over. The horse is guided not controlled. They are one, to face the universes problems together as equals. There is a confidence this produces that is palpable. But even Centaurs can still evolve and learn.

Both the horse and rider have its own unique way to mature and learn. And thus each of the four Types has its own unique way to mature and learn. For the rider, objective proof "convinces" it of reality. For the horse, personal experience "convinces" it of reality. But when balanced and trusting each other, the horse and rider can convince each other to efficiently move towards a common goal rather than wasting energy that saps them both.

The usual pattern of behavior between the horse and rider is one of action and reaction with cascading tensions broken by short periods of calm.

In real life, the rider pulls on the reins, agitating the horse, which then becomes more anxious, causing the rider to pull harder on the reins, which irritates the horse further, which causes.... A lot of time your horse is under this tension and you don't even realize it. It is subconscious. We say we are "ok" but underneath is this undercurrent of apprehension and tension that is constantly sapping our available energy. Sometimes we sense it and do something to alleviate it and it feels better for a while. But there is always more tension under that. You will never know when your horse is at its calmest.

We as humans often store this tension in various sites in our bodies. A couple of them are the jaw muscles (clenched), the cheek muscles in the face, and the neck and shoulders. Others grind their teeth at night to express their torturous inner turmoil from the horse-rider conflict. Naturally there is less tension and stress if you are more integrated. Also, the Type 2's and 3's immatures feel a lot more of this tension as their component parts fight for supremacy rather than co-operation.

Even when there is a temporary reprieve from the tension which feels good because it is temporarily dealt with, that doesn't mean the system is back to full strength. We often make this assumption and assume that this is the new normal, forgetting what being at full strength was like and we end up sacrificing a part of us as we get smaller and smaller.

This incessant tension is like a horse at the start of a race. All primed and ready to go, ready to serve the rider. It is in its stance waiting for the starting gate to open. It is full of energy waiting to be released. Everything is at its peak. Everything is churning and shaking. And the starting gate never goes up. Ever. The poor horse has to deal with this. Is it any wonder the horse and rider are at odds? A lot of people live their lives in this state with the horse expecting to be neglected or abused for a "good cause" by the rider. And the rider has to brace against being bucked off or sabotaged by an emotionally reactive or unresponsive horse. Is it any wonder most people are neurotic? We are constantly under tension (except for brief moments of respite) which drains us and creates conflicts within ourselves whereby we become our own worst enemy.

But, instead of being our own worst enemy, we can become our own best friend. The goal is to know your horse on a "first name" basis and understand how it feels, and sense what it needs to be healthy. Similar to how a mother can immediately discern the difference between a cry of anger or hunger from her new born infant. You have to know your horse before you can become one with it. This process starts from the beginning.

After we are born, there is only body with little else. The horse then develops. We then progress to develop a rider. Since the horse forms before the rider, it will develop with a certain energy level. The rider, when it develops, then has to deal with whatever energy level or strength this is. Then there is either a horse or rider in charge as they didn't start balanced. This results in either the horse or rider establishing a dominance as a general trend. If the rider develops stronger first, that will accelerate the process of developing a strong horse as the rider can handle it. If the horse develops stronger first, then this will delay the rider's development as well as the horse's development, making it more difficult for the rider. This delays maturity of the unit as the rider must lead. This gives the Type 1's an early advantage in life. Though a strong horse can initially be seen as an asset because of its power but if it is not guided properly, the power can be wasted in non- productive pursuits.

A strong horse is an asset as well as a liability depending on the rider's strength. It is an asset because of its emotions and feelings but also a liability because of them. A strong rider is also a liability as well as an asset depending on the horse's strength. The rider can be controlling or too controlling. The horse also can be emotionally powerful or too powerful. So having a strong rider first helps the maturation process, especially if it acknowledges the horse. It speeds up the integration process if the rider leads and also understands the value and role of the horse.

But the optimum is a strong horse and rider that are integrated harmoniously (Type 2 or 3) as the amount of available energy and its efficient use can be maximized. There is the original amount of energy the horse rider system was born with and the amount that can be used from the efficient harmonious integration. When this coincides with maturity, the final result is a powerful Centaur that can achieve most of what it wants and also be satisfied with what it can't do. And it has the wisdom to distinguish between the two, gracefully.

When your horse and rider are calmed, energized and in agreement, their system is at its optimum. Magic results, if not miracles. The goal of this book is to teach you how to mature and integrate your horse and rider (the more mature and stronger the system, the less stress there is) so that reins are no longer needed. Then your horse and rider can become like the mythical Centaur. The horse and rider differences, when integrated, make the wise Centaur much stronger than each separate.

This maturing process which establishes balance doesn't have to take a long time. If you strengthen the rider with accurate knowledge and discipline, and an understanding of the values and uses of the horse, it will allow the horse to mature faster and permit detachment and non-reactivity to occur quicker. This doesn't mean they turn off feeling and become a zombie but rather deal rationally with feelings and not let them become a liability. Thus, anger becomes much less common. This knowledge teaches the rider to stop poking the horse so both can mature faster. The goal is to reintegrate what is already integrated, in a different way, thus producing a trust and respect with each other and a deeper maturity.

There is a famous quote that says, "God, grant me the courage to change the things I can, the patience to tolerate the things I can't, and the wisdom to know the difference." The courage comes from a strong, mature rider, patience from a mature horse and the wisdom comes from the Centaur. The Centaur is a required component to make the whole system work at the optimum. It realizes the parts need each other and how to best use them without one having to dominate. One of these ingredients without the other is not nearly as productive and sometimes destructive.

As the rider continues its pursuit of happiness by acquiring things, it relentlessly rules pretty much every moment of everyday life which shields us from "the immensity of reality". The horse believes something different. Immensity is cool. This could be one reason people like sports and particularly extreme sports. Under these conditions the rider is in command and clarity, single mindedness, and detachment are possible. By forcing ourselves, in extreme sports, to be fully engaged in the situation, we remove fear. The rider conveys to the horse, we are going to do this so you better help or else. Fear must not occur or it will be distracting. There is a joy, peace, and a feeling of "aliveness" that is almost indescribable. Then contradictory thoughts end and you can truly listen and feel, what a blissful state. Time dissolves into its true evanescent nature, and we can truly enjoy our experience. Sometimes to be truly alive and appreciate life, you can't be attached to life.

I have a saying that I came up with when I was young. The Universe wasn't built for my satisfaction but I might as well enjoy what it does give me. This acknowledges that the universe wasn't built for my satisfaction which is an ideal of the Centaur. The second part, that I enjoy what it does give me, is the realm of the horse. The two go together beautifully and produce a feeling of happiness. Accept and appreciate what is. That is all there is to it. Then the horse and rider can get along and be what they were designed to be.

All it takes to do this is a change of perspective. It is the easiest thing to do when in sync and the hardest thing to do when not in sync. This allows a spiritual experience to be integrated into the horse and rider worlds. Spiritual liberation is not a matter of hard work or achievement but rather a matter of insight. Life is said to be difficult by some. But when you truly Accept this as true, it no longer matters and life becomes not difficult. The fighting of this notion wastes energy. The answer to every problem lies in the problem itself. A spiritual-like awaking occurs when the horse and rider agree and a Centaur emerges.

Some people, particularly the goal oriented Type 1 and Type 2's, believe that happiness is found at the end of the road. This is a rider perspective. The Centaur realizes that if happiness can't be found along the way, it isn't going to find it at the end anyway. The Centaur has established a trust between horse and rider that makes it stronger than the component parts. He utilizes both at the proper time. The Centaur recognizes it is beneficial to sometimes let the horse make a decision about which way to go.

The Centaur's broader perspective on all things has profound ramifications. The Centaur can relate to both male and female perspectives. This skill makes a personal relationship more successful. It can relate better to any "apparently" opposite perspective. The Centaur's broader perspective also translates into increased capabilities for the horse, rider, and physical body itself. Emotions are felt deeper and richer by the horse. Rational ideas are understood quicker and clearer by the rider. The ability to tolerate pain, cold or hot temperatures, any physical attribute is expanded with the Centaur. So not only will the Centaur have a broader perspective on social issues and psychological matters but also it will be able to tolerate more on the physical level, sometimes to miraculous degrees.

And it will not only be able to just tolerate more, it will actually be able to expand on the capabilities of the body to maximize the body's potential and recharge the immune system. This helps medical miracles to happen. In the same way, on the other end, a person who is out of balance with horse and rider, say like a "spoiled" person, will have a lot of physical intolerances which will actually retard the person's physical abilities and immune system.

As an example of this principle, I was once walking on a cold day with my son, Brady. He was incessantly complaining about how cold it was and I pointed out that his constantly emphasizing how cold he felt was actually making him colder psychologically. If he stopped this, he would feel warmer. But taken to the next step, he could not only feel warmer psychologically but also physically, by expanding his body's tolerances and then its actual limits to withstand cold. Naturally there are limits to this, given each individual body, but you can use this to maximize each individual body. And each Type has its own unique way to achieve this.

This idea can be used in general, more so by Type's 2 and 3. This promotes the skill to become a generalist. The more you do this in all things the more you are able to tolerate and deal with other things and become a generalist. (Omnivores rule over herbivores and carnivores because they are generalists) This diverse approach also allows one to adapt to problems, in general, rather than just having to avoid them. Spoiled people aren't generalists. They tend to be Type 1 or 4 immatures. Think about why .

A major benefit of "Centaur-hood" is a return to what made our species great, being a generalist rather than a specialist. This is a skill that can be relearned.

The rider, since civilized times, rides roughshod over the horse and body, preaching specialization as being more efficient and "better". The rider has to learn to share willingly the guidance over the organism. It has to trust and value the other parts of the system. Diversity wins in the end as most efficient.

As an aside, in order to give a little historical perspective to the Centaur, I will mention how the Centaur has progressed over time. We started out, as a species, as being all horse, same as in the growth of a single member of our species. As civilization developed, due to the rider, the rider moved toward preeminence. You could say the rider created civilization. By the time of the Greeks it was developed enough to prove its ideas could take over the world. The Greeks learned the power of the rider but also started to understand the benefits of the integration with the horse. Curiously enough, the Greeks invented the Centaur and incorporated it into their mythology.

The Romans then showed the power of an integrated horse and rider (but with more of an emphasis on the tyrannical nature of the rider) but both these cultures were more of a Level 1 integration as the integration was awkward, but more effective and powerful than anything else at the time.

With the advent of the Renaissance, the Artist/Scientist showed the true power of a well-integrated, strong horse And rider. Da Vinci was an example of a man who could paint the Sistine Chapel and design a helicopter. The Artist/Scientist is the generalist I spoke of earlier, The Centaur. All great human innovations and ideas are due to these type of people, the Centaurs. They can harmonize opposites and unite the horse and rider. To them, knowing truth meant being able to accept mutually incompatible viewpoints. Einstein is another more modern example of the same type of individual. They combine Art with Science to create miracles.

So throughout history, the Centaurs have led us as a species. But with the advent of the Industrial Revolution, the rider became dictatorial and decided the horse had nothing of real value to offer so it was there only to be exploited. The rider rose at the expense of the horse and thus Art and Science became opposites which despised each other. They became antithetical. Today there aren't a lot of Artist/Scientists but only Artists OR Scientists. Thus a lot of wisdom of the generalists has been lost. We lose things with "OR" and gain things with "And". This is an advantage of the Types 2 and 3 over the Types 1 and 4, and where the true wisdom of the Centaur shines through.

A mature trust between horse and rider can be called wisdom. This allows for less conflict and increased available energy (and less stress) that allows for greater flexibility, resilience and strength to promote a better attitude and broader perspective to respond to the vagaries of the universe. The major difference between an ordeal and an adventure is perspective. I define the increase in available energy as producing the feeling of happiness. And that happiness is a by-product of something else. So, the natural state of a mature horse and rider is happy. Thus, it is possible for us to live "happily ever after".

Peace can also be found here, because happiness is defined as abundant available energy, and happiness is just peace in motion. Peace is achieved by calming the internal battle between horse and rider. Peace from the incessant thinking thoughts of the rider that usurp our lives and attention. Achieving peace, happiness and freedom (from our selves) are the goals of this book. Also, personal relationships and love, as relating to horse and rider, will be discussed in Chapter 5 as a basis for achieving the goal of an integrated, fulfilling personal relationship as a "Centaur". Thus, you can user the horse-rider model in the real world for practical benefits.

As an example of how the horse-rider system works in the real world, I offer a real life incident which happened with my son, Brady, a Type 1, (who was age 14 at the time) and my daughter, Jessica, a Type 4 (who was age 10 at the time) at Lake Powell. I was trying to get them to jump off a 10 foot high cliff into the lake. I showed them by demonstrating the procedure and the fact that they wouldn't die doing it. After many failed attempts, Brady decided he couldn't do it. His horse, convinced he was going to die if he did it, overruled his rider who said he wouldn't die if he did.

The next year we went back and I gave it another try as he said he was determined to jump off the cliff. This time I again demonstrated by example that he wasn't going to die.

As I was floating in the water below I watched the epic battle unfold above as his horse fought with his rider to decide what he was going to do. He acted like he was going to jump, then at the last second he stopped. This went on for 15 minutes and I was amazed as I watched this internal struggle for control. Finally he jumped and when he came up he said that it was fun but scary. So I told him to try again. At this point I ask the reader to take a second to ask themselves to guess what the outcome was when he tried again......

90% of the people I polled about this said he would jump in quickly as he learned he wouldn't die. Well, he did the exact same thing as the first time. Finally he did jump again. But the important point is not the story itself, which is instructive anyway, but rather the fact that most people believed he would jump quickly. Thus demonstrating that most people really don't know how their own horse learns.

The horse does not respond to logic or rationality. The fact he survived the first attempt meant nothing to his horse the second time. The horse learns by repetition. It actually took 6 or 7 times before he felt comfortable doing it. I told him that when I jumped, my horse and rider were both on board so I enjoyed it more than him. His horse took a while before they were in concert in him. He felt fear until his horse was on board.

What actually happened internally with Brady was based on the fact that he is a Type 1 rider orientated, but he also had an immature or weak rider. He examined the cliff with his rider and assessed the pros and cons of doing it. Yes, I survived and he probably would also, but he also assessed a danger due to the height of the cliff. This concentrating on the cons (much like his cold weather experience) got his horse involved and anxious, to the point where his horse reared up and said, "No". Then he had to deal with an anxious and fearful horse. This then became the bigger problem, making the first problem much more difficult to solve.

Metaphorical horses are calm in general but also very fearful when anxious, just like real horses. This is not surprising since both animals have spent much of their history as prey and this had survival value.

Brady's rider had to deal with his anxious horse and he had to try to calm it down to the point it could be controlled. It is far easier to deal with a powerful horse prior to it getting riled.

Overcoming fears is one thing, it is quite another to do it gracefully, which can only be done when the horse is in agreement with the rider. The rider can control the horse's fear, but it is much easier if there is no fear to begin with. Understanding the role of fear in general is critical to calming the horse and requires a strong rider. Learning when and how to let go of fear is a life skill worth mastering. I have a saying that demonstrates this principle. Letting go changes everything because letting go changes nothing. Empty yourself till you are whole. Letting go requires courage. Think about this for a few months and the realization alone could change your life. It's all just perception or perspective. We determine reality. Thus we can change reality. What a powerful tool. Almost like God. Changing perspective is how we evolve or Integrate. It's a skill required to become a Centaur.

The Lake Powell story demonstrates a few principles concerning horse and rider. For one, Jessica, who was also with us, jumped the first time after only a very short time. But she is a horse oriented person (Type 4 immature). Her rider just said, "Dad did it and he said it is ok." The horse never got riled. Her rider trusted my rider's assessment.

Everybody has both horse and rider elements within themselves. How one responds to fear is one example of how the balance is manifested. The rider orientated people are more cautious. So they learn about life and experience it in a different way. Sometimes one perspective, or Type, has an advantage over other Types and sometimes it does not. But what if you could integrate both perspectives and use the best of both instead of the two fighting to see who dominates.

As an interesting aside, to be discussed later, most literature, books, movies, etc. have stories and characters that highlight horse versus rider conflicts. The interplay between them fascinates our horse and rider. If you take the time and examine favorite plots of stories, as well as people you know, you will find horse and rider elements embedded in almost any relationship and played out over and over again. It is fractal.

Take the old Star Trek series for example. Spock is a rider orientated character (Type 1) and Dr. McCoy is a horse type character (Type 4) while Captain Kirk is a blend between them (Centaur). We delight in seeing how these different elements that we find in ourselves play out in different genres and scenarios. We look to see if we can find answers about how they relate so we can use them personally. We see the advantages that the Spock character has with his logic, but we also see his limitations. Likewise with McCoy, we feel the thrill of his emotions, but also see his limitations. But Kirk fascinates us the most, as he seems to have found a way to integrate the two personae, a Centaur, to achieve success in fighting the universe's trials and tribulations.

These types of characters are rampant in literature as we seek to find ways to harmonize them in ourselves as well. We sense intuitively that we must find a way to do this to be in harmony. Harmony that gives rise to feelings of contentment with ourselves. Without this we are not balanced and everything in life seems black or white instead of color. Again, black "or" white is not the same as black "and" white which metaphorically produces color.

Not only does this theme occur in movies and literature but it also explains attraction in male-female relationships, not to mention the high divorce rate, as we seek the opposite in a mate because it fulfills a lack, but doesn't supply the need for the known. Differences between male and female horse and riders attract initially but similarities produce longer lasting results. However, a mixture of the two is the most successful formula. A detailed discussion of horse and rider personality traits that relate to relationships and love are left to Chapter 5. After an understanding is developed of horse and rider interplay, it becomes easier to understand why most relationships fail, and how to assist ones in trouble.

I repeat here, please be assured that I make no distinction about horse or rider being "better" than the other or any Type being better than the other. They are merely different. I also use the word "immature" a lot. But I don't use it with a negative connotation. Meaning "immature", in my view, is just undeveloped and that isn't a "bad" thing. Some people are more mature or stronger than others but a baby isn't "bad" because it happens to be immature and doesn't know how to walk yet. It is simply undeveloped.

The horse and rider are not opposites, just different. There is a big difference between "opposites" and "different", usually created by the rider. The rider creates opposites artificially, as horse and rider each has positives and negatives. The thesis of this book is that the important point of the venerable Chinese concepts of Yin and Yang is not Yin nor Yang but the word in the middle, without which neither could exist. And that is AND. "And" means diversity and balance, and balance is everything. At the balance point there is greatest diversity, the most of each. Integration at this point is the key. Expand your And.

I think everyone has an intuitive feel for the distinction between horse and rider. For instance, I ask the reader to make a determination of the type of author writing this book. You don't know me well but just the style I am writing this book in gives it away. I am a classically trained scientist taught to stay within the "box". I can write expository and dry but I am equally as comfortable with a more informal, verbal style. Written words are the "inside the box" realm of the rider, and spoken words are more the realm of the horse. The horse lives outside the box. But the maturing and reintegration of your horse and rider, the thesis of this book, allows one to make the very box disappear.

Author's usually have to decide what style to write their books in, more horse or more rider. I chose (not really much of a choice) horse orientated (unstructured) And rider oriented (structured) as I wish to talk to people's horses and riders. Riders relate to riders, as they experience reality the same way. The horse relates to other horses in the same way, as they are a herd animal. If you want to alter your world view you have to go to the horse. Your rider made you want to read this book and learn about the idea, but it's the horse that will change your life. See how they go together beautifully when balanced and integrated.

Btw, one of the reasons I use the horse/ rider metaphor is because I used to own a horse stable and personally witnessed many events involving horse and riders. So you folks with horse riding experience will feel particularly in sync with some of these ideas. Some of these ideas come right from the horse's mouth.

I also used to teach at a University when I was young and my style of teaching epitomized my beliefs even at age 22 when I started teaching. I believed, and still believe, that everything should be a blend of education and entertainment. One without the other is one dimensional. Education AND entertainment are the horse AND rider together. Curiously enough, students respond best to this mixture.

As an example of this, I was once teaching a lab in a Physics class with the students approaching the lab with the usual perfunctory lack of interest that students are sometimes known to exhibit. I decided to experiment with them to see if I could get them out of their cold, rider approach to the lab. So I told them to take all the lab equipment they were using on the lab table and put it all on the floor. There was a rug on the floor of this particular lab. Almost immediately, they got "into" the lab. The unstructured, casual, different approach to the experiment brought out the "horse" and they began rolling around on the floor to get better views of the experiment. They began to actually enjoy the lab. The horse's appearance allowed this to happen. There were different styles of responses from different individuals based on what Type they were and level of integration of course. But the main point was the integration of the horse and rider allowed then to get "into" it. Good teachers know how to bring the horse out in students.

Now, different people are born with different kinds of horses (some have a Clydesdale and others have Thoroughbreds). One type of horse can dominate more than the other. I have mentioned a little about when horse or rider dominate (designated - + and +- in the following graph) but sometimes they are both present in balanced proportions (designated ++). When these people are born with high energy they are charismatic. They can become dictators or presidents (mature or immature), demonstrating the power can be used for good or bad, i.e., Kennedy and Clinton or Hitler and Stalin. If you have high energy, a strong horse and rider, with integrated with maturity, then you have the most powerful combination possible, a Centaur. How the average person's life unfolds is determined by their Type and Integration Level.

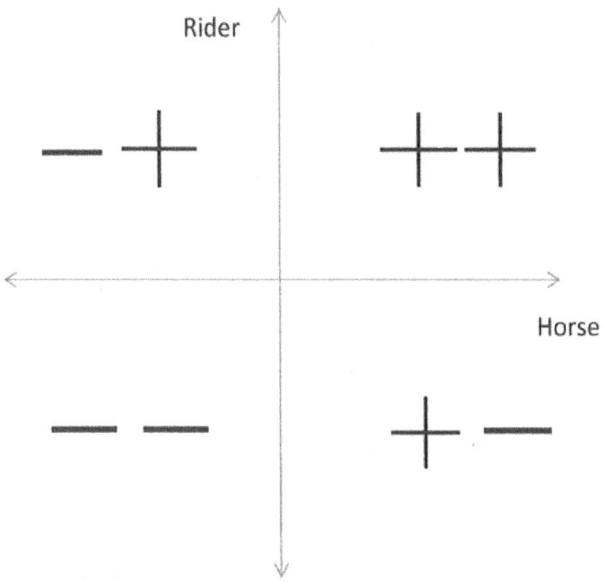

People who emphasize the horse component (Type 4) might become artists or musicians as a career choice. Again if you have this style with maturity and energy then they become some of the more successful variations in the group. People who emphasize the rider component (Type1) might become disciplinarians, academics (teachers), police officers, politicians, (any authority figure) or accountants.

Some people are born with low energy (minus, minus), they have a low energy rider, low energy horse. They go with the flow accepting what comes along with no real urge to change. They don't really care why anything happens. They just exist. They have not developed horse or rider. They are all body, not much horse or rider. Thus they appear to have very little "personality".

Now, within each Type, the horse and rider have the potential to mature. A rider could be just an immature rider, like in kids. Btw, kids are basically horses when really young and their rider develops as they grow, just like it did with our species. Adolescents, well everybody knows about them, they usually have lots of energy with a narrow perspective as they have an immature rider. Strength is gained by integration. Weakness or immaturity is simply non integration. A bully may appear strong, due to high energy, but he is actually weak in that he is mostly rider and not integrated, same thing with a geek, who generally are lower energy. They appear weak only because they have not integrated the horse yet. They act first and are often surprised when there are repercussions to their actions.

There are ways to mature a horse which makes it stronger and these will be talked about in coming chapters. But the point I want to make here is the various ways they can go together. And the main idea is that you can have a high energy or low energy horse that you are born with, but the expression of this can change when there is sufficient available energy coming from the conclusion of the horse and rider conflict. And when this available energy is used in agreement between the horse and rider, then good things happen. When horse and rider agree on a destination things go smoother and Integration becomes easier.

As an example of how this happens in real life, I was once on a horse ride where I was turned around in the saddle talking to a person behind me. The reins were loose and I wasn't really paying a lot of attention to my horse (Type 4, haha) as I trusted him to follow the path. Well, a bear popped out of the woods ahead of me and spooked the horse. Ordinarily, I would have ended up on the ground but I snapped the reins back in time to regain control. But the point is that once a horse spooks there isn't much left to do but hold on. If I saw the bear first I would have snapped the reins and established more control before the horse saw it and I would have a better chance of preventing the horse from spooking. I also have learned not to over react and panic when the horse reacts.

A vigilant mature rider has a better chance of controlling the horse. This also points out the extreme example of who has control in an emergency situation. The horse usually has the final say. (Oddly enough it can also has the first say if it chooses to) The rider appears in control but in actuality the horse is stronger than the rider. Is it any wonder the rider is terrified and controlling most of the time as it is outgunned and beaten to the punch most of the time.

The rider bluffs the horse into believing he is stronger but if the horse calls the bluff, watch out. But there are times, if the rider is strong enough, he can make the horse do almost anything. I have personal experience of this. When I was 23 years old I was teaching college, managing a real estate business, and going for a Master's degree. My rider ran my horse so ragged I ended up with cancer and was told I only had a year to live. Nothing left to do. The only way the horse/body had to slow me down (to get me to listen) was to kill me. Well turns out I turned down the chemo route and used my horse's energy and rider's knowledge to deal with it myself, plus some visualization techniques and other mind control ideas. But the point is that I put the horse and rider together and it created a miracle. I am not recommending this path for everybody. It is only one example of the possibilities, and it requires the presence of the Centaur.

Let's talk about miracles here. Parts of this book will resonate with the horse and other parts will resonate with the rider. This part will resonate with the horse. Nowhere else in human experience is the horse, rider and body components more appreciated, loved and revered than when they are frolicking in harmony.

In gambling it is called being "on a roll". In sports it is often described as being "in the zone". The horse is "harnessed" in the service of performance. The horse is not just controlled, fearless and calm, but energized for the challenge. This expands our abilities past our usual physical limits. This zone feels so joyful because we are utterly absorbed by it, our awareness is integrated with actions, horse integrated with rider. We sense only a narrow range of perception, totally focused on what we are doing, forgetting ourselves and all else. We become relaxed and focused. No straining or self-consciousness. It is similar to sexual love (not infatuation). Worry or anxiety are its opposites, if they enter, the spell is broken. We perform at our peak or beyond, like when in love, and the sheer pleasure of the act itself drives us. It is the "be and end all" because we get to just "be" and "end all" else. We are Free. Free to devote all our attention and energy to only One thing. While in the zone we are not concerned how we are doing or what we look like. The experience is all there is. Notice how your own horse is paying particular attention to this section as it knows we are talking about its realm.

Curiously, while in the "zone" people display masterful control of what they are physically doing. They are in harmony with the act. The focus is totally on the challenge. There is total concentration, like on a loved one. The horse becomes as focused as the rider, and more importantly, the horse becomes focused on the same thing as the rider. But there is no emotional static or fear, rather a calm type of focused emotion. This is the realm of the integrated, balanced horse and rider in tune.

There is a fundamental difference between love and infatuation. In love the horse calms down, so the rider can pull on the reins and the horse responds. In infatuation, the rider holds on for dear life, as the reins don't work. There is too much uncontrolled energy. It is out of tune.

You might think that being "in the zone" would take more energy but it actually takes less. It is the most energy efficient. Straining or worrying is what drains energy. The balance between horse and rider is critical. Too little rider and people become bored. Too much horse and they become anxious or obsessed. But when we reach that mystical state of balance, we can perform just beyond our bodily limits. We also have to develop some skill for the sport in question. The horse/rider can only take you as far as your body's skills allows. But the horse and rider have to be both in balance, each fulfilling their role together. The rider is integral to the process even if he is doing nothing, particularly if he is doing nothing.

A seesaw is a good example of this principle. It teeters from two extremes through a balance point in the middle. The system is infused with energy and the seesaw changes from one extreme, say the horse, through a balance point to the other extreme, say the rider. The balance point (sometimes called the Self) is in the zone where there are equal amounts of the two extreme points, the point of maximum diversity of the two. But it stays at the balance point only a moment before leaving. By managing the scale of the "teeters" we can stay longer at the balance or harmony point. But this point is never static or the system would be stuck and thus broken.

There is a comfortable range of motion, I call it the delta T of the system where maximum diversity and maximum productivity are located. This is the zone we are seeking to live in. And remember we never stay too long at the extremes one way or another. Perhaps the best way to remember this principle applied to real life is to say that nothing too good or too bad lasts too long.

But to get into this zone is the trick. You have to have a commitment to be so focused. Your rider has to be calm and energized. This takes some discipline. But once this is accomplished, (and the Centaur does this) emotional turbulence ceases and the sport becomes effortless. This is achievement without effort, which fills one with a sense of awe (Achievement

Without Effort). Sounds a little silly at first, but if you have ever played sports you know what I mean. The horse is free to tap into that cosmic energy source that defines it. It feels like you can't miss when shooting baskets. Everything seems easy. Time stands still. There is only the "now". This is harmony. This is balance. Ego disappears. You disappear and things happen as if by magic.

You feel the power of what it is like to be a Centaur. The rider loosens the reins and thought disappears, replaced by a new concept. It is not induced by thought. It is "the second before thought occurs". In this magical, wonderful moment all the energies of the psyche are harnessed and all possibilities are still possible, even medical miracles. I know you feel a version of "it" when you read this section. Everyone has had a taste of this but few explore this world fully. There is a door to the metaphysical world outside the box, and this book offers the key. It is the world of beauty filled with the mystery of intuition, when we know things without knowing why or how. It is where intuition and creativity coexist, the world of the Centaur. All creativity originates here. It is the essence of creativity in art, music, and everything else.

And the rider has to learn to correctly recognize the horses intuition gathered from this world, and when to trust it and when not to. This is also when we are most lucky. Understanding how this process works reveals the rules of luck and how to foster it. Yes, you can even create it.

It is the moment of creation in Art and Music when we produce more than we possibly are capable of. It is one of the most sublime and beautiful moments in life, like love. We are unified with it all. We are said to be "in the flow". When you are in the flow, you become part of the flow, becoming one with it. There is nothing but the flow. The Centaur lives and delights in this harmony. This is enlightenment and we all have experienced this effect to some degree and its delicate balance. Again, sometimes the rider's greatest contribution to the balance is to do less, to allow it to occur. Sometimes to do this requires it unlearn something instead of learning. Knowing when to loosen the reins is part of knowing when to tighten them. Horse and rider in sync is a magical thing.

There are two pictures here of a horse and rider in sync. I asked two of my friends about what kind of photo I should use to demonstrate this notion. My rider orientated friend (Type 1) suggested one and my horse orientated other friend (Type 4) suggested something different. I suppose by now you can guess who suggested what. One is playing polo (the rider's idea of sync as it occurs in the guise of a game of rules and beautiful control of the horse). The other is a native American boy riding full gallop, bareback, with the horse's mane flying in the wind and the boy sharing the exhilaration the horse feels, again perfect sync. Just of a different kind.

The horse contrasts with the rider. The fast mode of perception of the horse trades accuracy for speed. The rider provides accuracy. Together, in harmony, they are awesome. Separate, they can be trouble. The horse's intuitive quick judgment and emotions have liabilities as well as assets. Luckily, the horse has only moments of extreme emotion that are usually brief. But when these feelings are experienced for a longer period of time it becomes a mood which is easier to deal with, or when they are experienced longer still, it becomes a personality trait.

But often the horse/body is most noticed when emotions are in full heat. Aggression and depression, to name a couple, are due to reactive horses. In males, stress is often manifested outward as anger or aggression while females generally express stress inwards as depression which is anger expressed in a more socially accepted way. This is probably why females are more than twice as likely to suffer from depression as males. Thus, horses are more subject to depression than riders. Depression is when things seem to happen to us rather than by our desire. The universe seems overwhelming and unmanageable. Horses act without rider supervision. Feelings become self-justifying, assuming the guise of reason unless examined by the experienced rider. The rider must find a horse method, using the horse, to get out the horse out of this vortex. Again we see the differences between horse and rider as good or bad, however, when harnessed and merged the results are undeniably harmonious and magical; like a song sung in tune instead of out of tune.

Parts of this book will resonate with the horse and other parts will resonate with the rider. This part talks to the rider. A runaway horse with no reins can be dangerous. Infatuation is an example of what can happen to a horse if left unguided. Also, the body needs guidance to help avoid addictions, particularly with an immature rider. So, let's talk rider for a minute. The rider's realm is inside the box. Knowledge gives control and discipline. Knowledge permits us to anticipate the future and to take advantage of it or at least prepare for it. Knowledge gets us to the moon.

There was a study done by Walter Mishel in 1972 involving marshmallows and kids. The project leader offered kids a choice between having one marshmallow right away or waiting till he returned, 15 minutes later, when they would be given two marshmallows. Discipline was required to delay gratification for better future gain. Most children lasted about 6 minutes before munching the treat in hand. The study found that the longer the kid waited before eating it, the better they did academically and socially. This is a valuable skill to master.

A variation on this same skill was learned by Brady at the cliff at Lake Powell. To eat or not to eat a marshmallow is basically the same decision as to jump or not to jump as both involve the horse trusting the rider to accurately assess the situation. Horse and rider must act together for the good of the person. The horse trusting the rider's mature knowledge and judgment. I might mention the outcome of the marshmallow study would have been quite different if the kids didn't trust the experimenters. If the experimenters were known to the kids to be untrustworthy, i.e., they wouldn't really get the two marshmallows when they came back, then the kids would have not waited at all. Trust is the key. I leave it to the reader to decide if the kids who did wait the longest for the two marshmallows were rider oriented or horse oriented.

As a further example of the principle, when I was 19, I was asked by peers to try alcohol. I had some knowledge of the pros and cons. I saw the benefit of fitting in and loosening up. I saw the pain and consequences of the next day. I decided to try a couple of drinks and stop. A friend of mine confronted with a similar situation later became an alcoholic and drug user.... To jump or not to jump that is the question...To eat a marshmallow or not to eat that is the question...Does the horse follow the rider? Does the horse trust the rider? Should it? The answers, to a Centaur, are easy.

The power and energy of the horse is useless to the rider unless he finds a way to focus it toward something. The rider wishes to create productivity and accomplishments. It's how we got to the moon. Knowledge of our universe by learning about the physical laws that govern it, allows for those very laws to be used to the rider's advantage. For instance, the mature rider knows the sun will come up every day if we worship it as a religion or not. Knowledge is power. Understanding is power. It allows for the idea to explore the next pasture for new grass. The novel, the new, is in the realm of the rider. Knowledge allows for assessing probabilities of potential new threats and benefits. The known is the realm of horse. They like things to stay the same.

The novel or known can both be dangerous so assessing the probabilities of each is best left up to the Centaur. Both the horse and rider possess unique tools that can be merged together to deal with the vagaries and trials of the universe, instead of fighting between themselves.

CHAPTER TWO

The important part of Yin and Yang is not
Yin or Yang but the And in the middle

So I've talked a lot about the horse and rider and their various attributes. I hope you have a feel for the components of the psyche which are interesting by themselves but the fireworks really begin when they interact. Metaphorically speaking, life is a series of events concerned with creating fire, using fire, and putting out fires.

As you all have surmised by now, the horse rider system is a love-hate relationship because the horse doesn't generally understand the rider and vice versa. They are apples and oranges to each other (even in some Type 2 and 3's) and they talk apples and oranges, all the while expecting the other to understand. Is there a wonder there is a problem? There is this constant tension between your horse and rider over how to deal with themselves and how to deal with the universe so that they both get their desires dealt with, and the universe's problem as well. This creation of tension can take two different directions.

Sometimes, the rider is in charge and causes problems and sometimes the horse is in charge and causes problems. The relative size of the problem is a reflection of the relative strengths of the horse and rider. Let's look at two possibilities.

The first possibility occurs when your rider is dominating and the horse reacts to the rider. Examples include such events as not yelling at your boss (submitting to an authority figure). Your rider recognizes that resources may be lost by yelling at the boss so it uses discipline to restrain the horse. Yanking on the reins forces the horse to comply, so as to not allow the horse voice its opinion that the boss is being a horse's ass (Sorry about that). The horse wants to freak out because it wants to let the boss know it feels but the rider is preventing it.

The use of discipline is a prime indicator of the rider's control of the horse. The horse doesn't always respond well to it. There are many examples of this kind of tension in our culture. Almost limitless examples; Staying together for the kid's sake; Having to make the house payment so you don't go on vacation; "Big boys don't cry".

Your horse wants to express itself and it is not allowed to by the rider or culture, producing tension. In our society, which is heavily rider biased, the horse most often loses out. A major part of our society glorifies the rider and often vilifies or just ignores the horse. This produces escalating tension because the rider usually uses more discipline when the horse reacts, forcing a more extreme reaction from the rider, etc.

It is interesting that Hollywood exists because of this. Hollywood glorifies the horse because it is repressed elsewhere. Hollywood is an outlet for the need of the horse to be expressed. It lets the horse go on a romp vicariously because we can't or won't let our horses do the things we see on the screen.

As an historical example of this principle, look at the 1960's culture (Type 4) versus the Victorian culture (Type 1). In the Victorian period we had great literature and poems. It was a very repressive period in history, and rider orientated, but also one of the most prolific in literature because the horse had to be expressed, one way or another.

The 1960's was a period when the horse was expressed in an unrepressed culture. There wasn't any great literature produced in this period because the horse was not repressed. The angst to create wasn't there. Also, as a parallel, consider the 1950's culture versus the 1960's culture. The 50's were, in general, conformist, rigid, follow the rules, restrained and pretty much rider orientated. The 60's were freedom orientated, spontaneous, free flowing, uninhibited and pretty much horse orientated.

It is even possible to distinguish between the two stereotypical personae of the eras by their dress as well as hair length. The 50's riders were short haired, conformists, and neat while the 60's horses were long hair, wild, and different. This went pretty much for guys as well as girls. It is interesting that you can almost physically identify a horse versus rider personality before they even open their mouths.

Getting back to the two possibilities for creating problems, the second possibility is when your horse is in charge and the rider has to take a back seat. Examples of these are addictions, infatuation, greed, lust, crimes of passion etc. Infatuation, for example, is where the relationship is everything. It trumps all. It feels so good you do almost anything to perpetuate it. You sacrifice even yourself to feel the rush, thrill, the almost cocaine like high of seeing or thinking about that special person. The fact that the person might have an obvious flaw (say the person is in prison) that prevents the relationship from realistically working doesn't matter. The situation is dealt with by a brief explanation which the horse believes is true. It doesn't matter that 2+2 =5. The horse says it feels good and it is going to do it. The rider yanks on the reins but they don't work. Here the rider freaks out, yanks hard, and is scared when the horse doesn't respond. The rider knows harm will result if it isn't listened to, but is helpless to do anything but watch. All he can do is hold on and hope for the best, that the horse will come to its "senses", which of course it has, ironically enough. If the rider reacts, it produces more tension as the horse uses more power to resist it, producing a similar effect as in the earlier story of the horses on the hill slope.

This reacting and re-reacting is wasteful and prevents creativity from occurring. It is the opposite of creativity. Creativity is when the energy of the horse and rider is additive in a constructive manner. It is constructive interference versus destructive interference. Reaction often leads to anger and other negative emotions. The ego becomes inflamed and attacks. And remember, an attack is just a demand for assistance. The reactive tension created then has to be discharged somehow.

But tension can be also discharged positively as in a creation of something, for instance, the creation of this book. I get frustrated seeing people unable to live up to their potential because of being reactive and this produced the desire to create this book to help. Let's just say there is a lot more reacting going on in the world than creating.

This tension produced by the rider poking the horse can waste energy as I have said. Most people are their own worst enemies because of all the civil war going on within them about how to deal copaceticly with the respective demands of the horse and rider. Then the universe steps in with a problem, any problem, and the psyche has to fight a war on two fronts. Is it any wonder people are exhausted? And that the universe seems so hostile and formidable. The major issue I wish to address here is how to empower people by giving them energy from the horse and rider system (by not wasting it) to deal with the universe. So the universe becomes your friend and not enemy.

This civil war plays itself out every day in many different ways in every part of our lives. It is ubiquitous. Sometimes we are aware of it sometimes not but it is always there. It is fractal. On a large scale, in our culture we glorify the rider's ability to win the war by glorifying capitalism, control, conformity, authority. Our culture is just the sum expression of the how each person deals with their horse and rider interplay, more about this in Chapter 6. On a smaller scale, it also explains how we treat our kids and our interpersonal relationships.

The way we treat our own horse is how we treat everything else in our lives. If you are rider based, then you are more of a disciplinarian with your kids, pets, etc. Some extreme examples of immature Type 1 rider based parents believe kids should be seen and not heard. Follow the rules. Conform. Control them. Tolerate little disobedience. If they get out of line, spank them. The more moderate members of this group try to instill discipline with a little more understanding. These are some examples of rider based parents but that is how they treat their own horse also. I think you can anticipate how each of the four personality Types I mentioned earlier would be as parents.

Then there are the horse based parents that are more tolerant of their kid's behavior. The immature Type 4 examples of these let their kids do anything they want. The more moderate members (Type 2 or 3) try to instill discipline with a little more understanding. They don't have to control everything about them. They believe more in letting kids be who they are and tolerating differences between them and their parents. The rules aren't as rigid. Conflicts aren't settled by "Because I said so." There is more of an attempt to explain to the kid's rider why they need to modify their behavior.

As an example of this, my son extracted his favorite pie from the fridge and asked me if he could have some. I said, "sure". He said, "How big of piece?". I said, "As much as you want." (My wife at the time said just cut him a right size piece.) He thought about it and cut a normal size piece. He knew that if he chose a huge piece he might not be granted the same right next time and he liked having autonomy over what he chooses. He also knew that choosing a real small piece didn't benefit his horse either.

Personally, I like the idea of teaching accurate rider judgment (more precisely, allowing judgment to be learned) rather than fixed rules of the rigid Type 1's, or fixed sizes of anything because it teaches kids to check in with their horse and rider's desires before making a decision. His horse said take all the pie. Curiously, if he chose this alternative and got sick, the lesson would have been learned anyway. What would have been learned by me cutting the pie for him anyway? That his judgment is untrustworthy? His rider concluded it was better off with something less. Sometimes, less is more, especially to a mature horse. This is a valuable lesson which allows the horse to mature. Also it prevented any escalating tension because the horse and rider both got some of what they wanted.

But this escalating tension can also exhaust both your horse and rider. How does nature deal with this? There is a question currently unexplained in Psychology. The average person needs about 8 hours sleep each night. But we only require 4 hours to physically recharge from the day. Why the extra time? Nobody knows. But I think it is to allow time for the horse and rider to be separated, to get a break from each other. Sleep is when the rider gets off the horse. The horse is left on its own, out to pasture. The rider feels safe that the horse can't hurt himself at night since the horse/body is immobile.

Nature actually promotes this by designing sleep paralysis into the human being. Sleep paralysis is when the body is paralyzed during sleep, the muscles won't function while one is asleep. That's why people often find they can't scream during a dream or they wake up unable to speak or move or a little while. This prevents the horse from "running away with the body" while dreaming which can be dangerous.

Dreams are the realm of the horse unfettered by the rider logic about how things actually are. Thus they don't have to make sense except to the horse. The horse is free to go over the days adventures and play out different or similar scenarios to what it should have done. The horse is trying to understand the world of the rider in horse terms. It is trying to comply and learn where it might have gone wrong. It is doing its homework to try to understand and comply next time. Dreams are learning experiences and often they teach us about how to deal with our fears, as well as how to get over those fears. Most dreams are themes on frustration. You want to do this or that but are thwarted by something. This is expressing the horses' lack of understanding and frustration about how to deal with all the "rules". The horse is searching for a way for it to understand how to deal with the rider reality so it can be helpful.

Upon going to sleep, the horse first deals with the most antagonizing elements of the day. Sometimes this produces nightmares, curiously, a mare is also a horse. After this is taken care of, the horse can now deal with its own problems and desires. So, if the horse is calm and at peace with the events of the day, it is unfettered to pursue its other interests. This is when "good" dreams result, like the ones where we are flying or finding treasure. It is a good indicator of a well- balanced horse. It has time for itself. The rider isn't demanding things of it.

Often times when we can't get to sleep it is because the rider is agitated and doesn't feel safe to "get off the horse". It is still trying to deal with the next day's trials and doesn't want to release control back to the horse. To solve this problem the rider must be calmed down. Often images of things that don't concern it can help to relax it. Think of silly things that don't involve the rider. Reading a book can do the same thing. The rider knows its abilities aren't required and it relaxes. It won't relinquish control until it feels safe to do so. If it is agitated this can be transmitted to the horse and a nightmare can result. It is very important, if you are having trouble sleeping, to relax the rider prior to going to bed. It is also important to wake up without over emphasizing the rider. Give the transition time to integrate without stress. Don't multi-task or do things that require stringent rider input. The less rider input before sleep, the easier it is for the rider to dismount.

It is also interesting to note that rider orientated people (Type 1 or 2) tend to have more nightmares than horse orientated people (Type 3 or 4). By now, this should be beginning to make sense why this is so.

Now, there is this concept of lucid dreaming. This is basically being aware you are dreaming. Some people have the capability to consciously change what happens in their dreams. So in this case, the rider is still with the horse but it is walking alongside the horse. In this stage of sleep the parietal lobe is activated (the conscious mind) and the dreamer is conscious but without senses. So consciousness itself does not depend solely on sensory input. In this state the rider is closest and most intimate with the horse's world and how it views things. Unfortunately, for most people, this is not very common as it would permit a more intimate relationship between horse and rider and facilitate their communication.

And then there is the matter of how to interpret what the horse dreams mean. The question should be, "What did it mean to the horse?" Interpreting it through a rider filter makes this incorrect or impossible, as he speaks a different language and the rider likes to interpret everything only in terms of the rider perspective. Interpreting dreams correctly only becomes possible after you understand the horse and its language. Then it becomes simple, just like the horse.

But the horse needs to be away from the rider and vice versa in order for them both to rest. The less sleep a person needs therefore indicates a better balanced horse rider system. It's interesting, and understandable, that riders (Type 1 or 2 people) seem to need more sleep than Type 3 or 4. Centaurs don't require a lot of sleep.

But most people are sleep deprived. What does this tell you? Even with a natural release to deal with it, we are all still exhausted. Is it any wonder alcohol and drugs are rampant in our society? Our horses are driven into the dirt by more and more urgent requests for energy and emotions. Horses require sedatives to just get by. Our riders pretend nothing is wrong and try to convince the horse of this. Humans are excellent at living in toxic environments pretending there are no ill effects, throwing the horse a bone now and then and calling it good. The horse wears down, the rider wears down, and there is no energy to correct the situation. And then we blame the universe for causing it. We get used to it and quietly lead lives of passive desperation. Most people are operating in debt literally as well as figuratively. They simply don't have the energy to deal with the universe.

They become pessimists and life seems hopeless and they give up. It's just not worth it. That's the bad news. The good news is that there is something you can do about it. There is a third choice besides shooting yourself in the foot and shooting yourself in the head. Integration develops energy to use to deal with the universe.

As an example of this, there are people who are always lamenting the fact that they are alone and can't find a mate. They spend a great deal of time sorrowful that there is nothing they can do and it feels terrible. Some people just don't want to exert the effort to change things. They feel nervous about possible failure and feel bad about that too. But they don't mind being alone enough to overcome the defense mechanism to preserve their ego. So while the say they are suffering from being alone, it is actually not as bad as all that because they gain something from avoiding the possible pain. When the pain of being alone is actually greater than the pain of failure, they will actually do something about it. The horse and rider are jockeying for position to decide which outcome prevails. It depends on the relative strengths of the horse and rider. People with a well-balanced, strong horse and rider don't usually have this type of problem.

So, we have seen how the horse and rider interact with each other and with the problems presented by the universe. There is a diagram I wish to present that describes a more detailed perspective on how this interaction occurs for any given angst, need or frustration (any problem) provided by the universe. For this discussion to be most accurate, I will separate the horse from the body, so there is now horse, rider and body.

It is based on the ideas I have mentioned. It is a graphical way to view it that appeals to the horse. As we travel around the great circle of life, the horse, rider and body encounter problems which they attempt to deal with in their own way. The riders approach to a problem consists of using its curiosity to examine a problem in an attempt to solve it. It then progresses from this to search its knowledge, and the knowledge available to it, in order to solve the problem. Using this knowledge, it seeks an understanding of the problem which it hopes will led to an acceptable answer that the horse and body will agree with. On this path there are pitfalls that resemble vortices. These are time consuming, energy wasting pits that delay the answer to the problem. The horse and body also have their own circles with their vortices they travel around in search of the answer. I have constructed a diagram to show this.

It is a big circle with exits, like on an Interstate highway. As humans travel along this path, they approach a need, angst, or frustration, or any problem for that matter. The rider can then choose to use its abilities to solve the problem, which leads it to exit the big circle into the rider circle in an attempt to solve the problem using rider ideals. He first uses his curiosity to seek knowledge about the problem. Hopefully this will lead to an understanding about the problem. This will then lead to acceptance as the problem is solved. This process can lead to an agitated horse who exits the big circle to enter the horse circle to deal with it using horse ideals (Feelings and Emotions). The rider, meanwhile, may exit the rider circle to become bogged down in a variety of rider vortices. There are a series of these possible pitfalls, including, to list a few, Distractions, Inaccurate Knowledge, Analysis paralysis, Denial, and Refusal to let go.

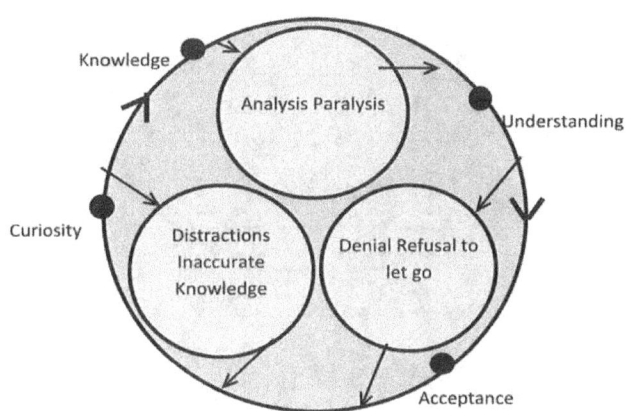

Rider Circle

They all can waste time and energy depending on the maturity and strength of the rider. This can agitate the horse.

The horse, meanwhile, is exploring the horse circle (Feelings and Emotions) to use its tools to solve the problem. It may exit the horse circle and become bogged down in any of the horse vortices, to list a few, (Anxiety, Depression, O.C.D., Emotional fears) which swirls it around as the horse flails against the problem. It rears, snorts and cavorts around in a whirlpool, not getting anywhere but just wasting energy.

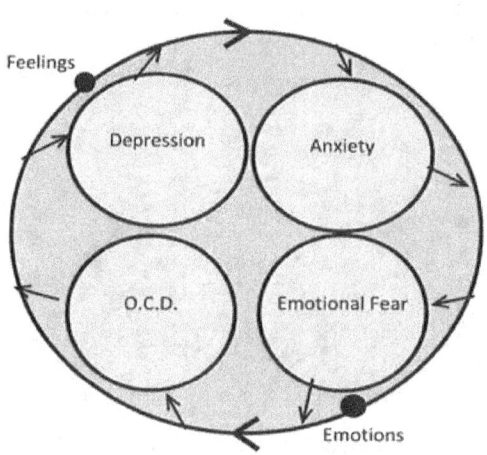

Horse Circle

The rider, seeing this, uses his toolkit of curiosity **to** seek knowledge, to gain understanding and an acceptable way to deal with the problem and calm the horse. Sometimes the rider, as it continues around the rider circle, gets caught in one of these eddying vortices. These vortices sap energy and time and curiosity is wasted on things like exploring diversions and distractions that don't help. Another vortex consists of useless accumulations of non-important or erroneous knowledge, like habitually searching websites you already visited, or etc.

Eventually the rider escapes this vortex and continues around the circle toward knowledge but it may take another exit into the vortex of analysis paralysis. Here there is constant mulling over the same thing with no different answer. This often manifests as incessant mind chatter or mental diarrhea. The rider wastes valuable time and energy here as it searches for the problem. Finally it comes out of this eddy and back on the circle until it hits Understanding. An answer from the knowledge quest has led to understanding the problem. This calms the rider. But just because the rider understands the problem, and a potential solution, doesn't mean the problem is solved. There is a vortex here he may take into Denial, or Fear of Letting go. It may understand but not accept the understanding to solve the problem. It may deny the understanding. It may have a fear of accepting the understanding. Finally, it may exit this vortex and proceed back to the rider circle. The next step is acceptance. This is where the rider accepts the solution to the problem and if the horse agrees, it calms the horse down.

The horse calms down to rejoin the rider at the acceptance point on the big circle. They both accept the solution to the problem. They can then proceed along the outer circle productively and with joined harnessed energy, until they confront the next angst, need or frustration. But if they approach this next problem still united, they may well avoid the exits and keep on the circle of life, missing the energy sapping vortices.

While all of this is going on, the body has its own circle pertaining to its interests and its way of solving the problem. Its world consists of instincts, energy, and a desire for sustenance. The body uses these to solve its problems. Its vortices consist of Physical fears, Physical illness, and Addictions, among others. The body can also be affected by the problem the rider is dealing with, as it uses its instincts and energy in an attempt to solve the problem. It also can fall into vortices. The body's solution to a problem may be alcohol. Also, physical illnesses may result due to the horse or rider stuck in their vortices. The universe itself may supply a physical illness to the body.

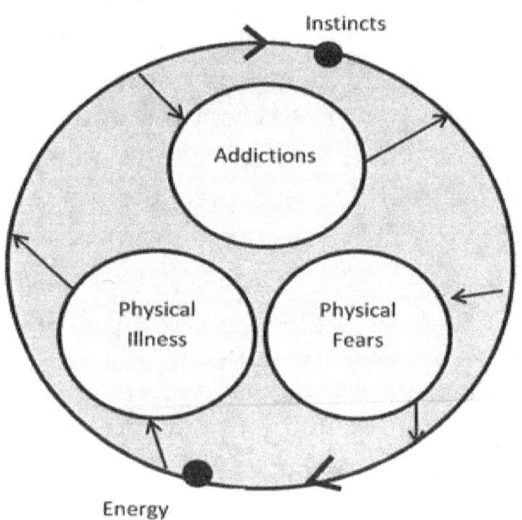

Body Circle

Similarly, addictions can result as the body searches for its solution to the problem. This can take the form of drugs, alcohol, etc. However, if the horse or rider finds a solution to the problem that the body agrees with, then the body rejoins the horse and rider on the circle of life and the team reunite. These vortices deserve a bit more explanation as people waste a lot of time and energy here.

When the horse/rider/body is in a vortex it is much harder for them to help themselves or help each other. Often times it can result in them fighting themselves. This is what I have been describing in the book. So, they all become much less productive or useful. If the body is in a vortex, the rider finds it harder to concentrate or focus. Thus he becomes a weak rider, causing immature traits to appear. When the rider becomes bogged down in a vortex he often can't shut himself up. Repetitive thoughts that never cease are a sign of a vortex. Thus he becomes non-productive, helpless, (his knowledge can't help) and sometimes destructive to horse or body. Sometimes the body can help extricate the rider from the vortex through exhaustion or sleep. We often can't get to sleep because we are worrying about a problem. But in the morning it doesn't seem so bad. This is because the rider isn't in the vortex in the morning. The rider is susceptible to these vortices because the rider believes he can solve any problem his way. The rider is stubborn. Type 1 and 2 immatures are very susceptible here. Immature riders can waste a lot of time and energy if not kept in check by the horse and body. It is much harder for the rider to be productive.

The horse also has its own problem with vortices. While in its vortex, it also can't help itself. This can drive the horse into the vortices of Anxiety, Depression, Obsessive Compulsive Disorder, Emotional fears etc. Anxiety is a result of the horse unsuccessfully trying to desperately use its ideas in an acceptable rider way. This leads to a look of insecurity, as insecurity is just what results when one "tries" to be secure. O.C.D. can also result when the horse tries to solve a problem mimicking rider methods, like compulsively washing the floor 5 times a day. This is the emotional horse trying to do a rider thing (keeping clean to avoid germs) and doing it repetitiously as a horse version of a solution. The rider says once is enough if done efficiently but the horse doesn't relate to efficiency so it does it repetitiously which it does relate to. It just can't tell when enough is enough.

The horse's approach can become a problem in itself. This also makes the rider's job harder to find a solution to the original problem as this becomes something else the rider must deal with (like Brady at Lake Powell). Similarly, the rider may have to deal with the body when it is in one of its vortices. Keep in mind the horse/body vortices are harder for them to get out of than the rider in rider vortices. Thus it is more important to keep the horse/body out of these vortices to begin with. Also keep in mind there are predispositions to fall into the horse/body vortices that are driven by the body and genetics.

The body can exit into its vortices from which it can't help itself, (the rider or horse must come to its rescue) like physical illness caused by the horse/rider or physical illnesses caused by the universe. All the while this is going on, the universe may throw in another problem to deal with. Also, the three entities still have to deal with each other while wallowing in a vortex. They can help each other to extricate themselves from a vortex or they can also help put one of the other members into a vortex. How this all goes together and manifests is dependent on what Type you are, how well integrated, and the strength of your and rider. If we combine these three circles into one large one, it would look like this:

Path to Centaur-hood

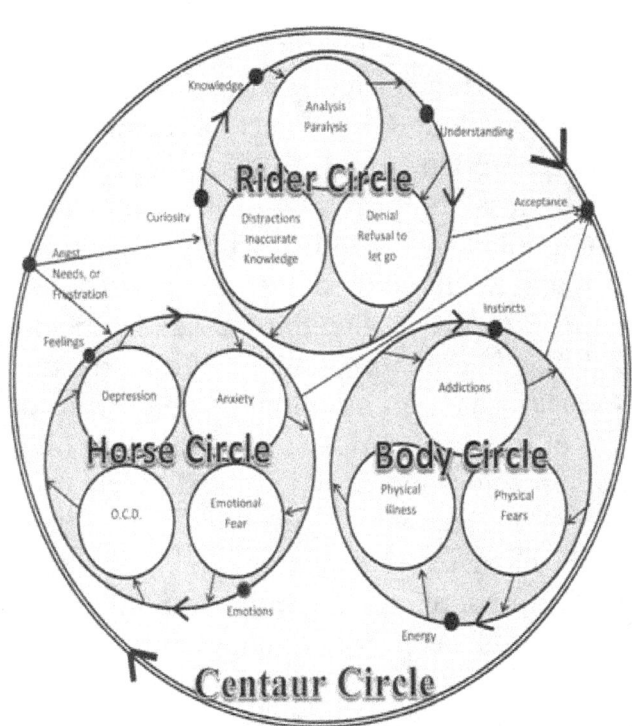

One can see pretty easily how the travels around the circle are highly dependent on the relative strengths or maturity of the horse and rider and which of the four personality types you are. Naturally, 1's and 4's take a lot different trip around the big circle than 2's or 3's. And by now I think you can see why. We will now look in detail at these trips.

Type 1's are very susceptible to the rider's vortices, and immatures spend a lot of their time here. They try to tough it out till they find a solution to a problem and insist the horse and body just shut up and sit still, till they find it. They use rider "override" to maintain control while they search for the answer using their methods. Type 1 matures spend less time in rider vortices due to their experience and broader perspective. Type 2's immatures spend a lot of their time in these rider vortices as they have the rider's desire of knowledge to solve problems but the emotional component makes them doubt and they sometimes miss an answer to the problem. Their horse component can be a distraction to their rider. A Type 1 mature will see the answer sooner with less distraction, and can be sometimes aided by the horse.

The Type 3 immatures don't often get stuck in rider's vortices as their emotional component doesn't see a lot of value in a rider's approach to solve the problem. So they give up on it quickly, choosing to look elsewhere (horse circle) for the solution. Type 3's and 4's are more likely to get bogged down in horse vortices like anxiety and depression. Similarly, Type 1 and 2's are less likely to get bogged down in horse vortices as they don't value answers found here. Mature Type 1's will also be less likely to fall into body vortices as they can override some of the body's suggestions. Type 3's and 4's will be more likely to fall into horse and body vortices as the horse and body are more closely aligned than horse and rider.

The Type 2's and 3's, being a blend, have ways to avoid/deal with the horse and rider vortices if they are integrated enough. Naturally the better integrated they are, the less likely they will fall into a vortex to begin with and be better able to extricate themselves and continue around the circle. The Centaur rarely falls into any vortex as his perspective grants him the ability to see the vortices early, avoid them, and save the energy for better things. He stays on the outer circle and builds up momentum to welcome the universes next problem, though he sees these problems as more of a learning experience than a problem, as an opportunity to advance further.

The relative strength of each horse and rider also figures into the preceding discussion. A strong rider has an easier and quicker time achieving acceptance and keeping out of vortices. As they get to know each other, the horse and rider try to classically condition a habit of avoiding the exits, thus further increasing their energies as they are not wasted. Thus making proper efficient choices to avoid wasting time and energy in the vortices is the goal.

The concept of making successful choices is important because it grants freedom. We are all a lot freer than we believe and we all have more choices than we believe. And having choices is fundamental to freedom.

For instance, take paying taxes. Do we all have a choice about paying taxes? A lot of people say "No" we have to pay them. And feel bad when they have to do it. But this isn't true. You don't have to pay them. You have a choice. You can go to jail or have a garnishment of your wages to pay them. If the cops show up at your door and say they are going to take you to jail unless you pay, you would say, "Here take the money and Thank you" and feel good about it. It's all perspective. A Centaur understands this.

We saw how the travels around the circle are highly dependent on the relative strengths or maturity of the horse and rider, and what Type they are. A person with a strong horse "and" rider has an easier time achieving acceptance and keeping out of vortices than a person with a strong horse "or" rider. (Or a person with a low energy horse or rider.)

Energy is another way out of vortices, as vortices are energy sapping and stressful in nature. But if one has sufficient energy (from the body) to begin with, you can use that to climb out of a vortex.

Let's take a little more detailed view of the travels around the circle in view of efficiency (how successful) and practicality. We will use a practical problem to show how the circles work in real life, like "Should I break up with my partner?"

The Type 1 immatures (very inefficient) would encounter the problem and attempt to bull their way through it with their limited perspective, all the while cursing the universe for putting any impediment in their way. They feel justified in being annoyed with reality. Their rider would think of all the logical reasons that their partner "should" stay with them, and why they should stay with their partner. They would not address any reasons why their partner shouldn't stay with them. Their rider analysis would only address the logistics and practical benefits of staying together. Their horse might exit the big circle into the horse circle but the rider is not overly concerned as it believes this is not a big problem (sometimes the rider doesn't even know it or admit it). The rider attempts to solve the problem, confident every problem can be solved by him alone, without the horse or body interfering. This rider will fall into the rider vortices. and spend his time there, considering if the practical benefits of the relationship are worth being concerned with. It is difficult for this rider to reach the acceptance point on the circle as he has difficulty understanding any emotional side of the problem. They often get stuck in endless, swirling, energy sapping vortices and are rarely able to integrate the horse into the problem. Thus delaying their journey to the promised land.

A Type 1 mature (more efficient) will have a different journey around the circle. They will confront the problem with the horse mixed into the equation but they will be less likely to exit into the horse or body vortices as they understand the horse and body better, thus making things easier to begin with. But if the horse does exit, then the mature Type 1 will be able to exit the vortices these quickly and continue in search of the answer. They will also be less likely to exit into the rider vortices and waste time there, and more likely to reach the acceptance point that is agreeable to its horse. So they will look at the rational and emotional reasons for staying together, giving proper weight to each, and make a successful decision. They are also less likely to have the horse exit the next time the same or another problem comes up. This increases efficiency.

The Type 2 immature's, when confronted by the problem, will be more likely than Type 1's to have the horse exit into the horse circle, and will be somewhat aware the horse has done this. The Type 2 will, first, use their curiosity and knowledge of the universe to try to find an answer to the problem using rational reasons but they will be also be able to use their horse component to assist in the problem so the horse will be less of a problem itself. They can fall into rider vortices, and it is likely they will stay there until they are satisfied that all the rational reasons have been analyzed. They will also briefly consider the emotional reasons for staying together, trying to choose which is the most valuable side to lean toward in answering the question, though, they usually suspect the answer. Their conflict may entail dragging the body into the question as their conflicts can cause the horse to get anxious which might cause the body to fall into one of its vortices. They also will be more reactive when falling into a vortex. The benefit of the Type 2 is a consideration of more variables to address the problem. But, they also have a good chance of falling into horse, rider and body vortices.

The mature Type 2's will have a decided advantage because while they consider more variables. They will be less likely to fall into vortices and will solve the problem much quicker and more successfully. The integration of the Type 2 mature's also reduces reactivity due to falling into vortices. Being highly reactive can make the vortices deeper and thus harder to get out of. The Type 2 mature can also use the horse to assist in overcoming the problem, providing the horse hasn't gotten too riled up about the problem which decreases efficiency. The immature Type 2's will have a tougher time here. If it is more of a horse orientated problem they will flounder longer in the rider circle and its vortices as they are not an expert in this area, thus decreasing efficiency. Some problems are more horse orientated and some are more rider orientated. The Type 2 mature thus has an advantage (more efficient) over the Type 1 and Type 2 immature; Less wasted time in vortices, less waste of energy, and less stress about the problem.

When the Type 3 immatures encounter the problem they will feel the horse exiting into the horse vortex more dramatically (less efficient). They will pay attention to this "exit" more acutely and deal with this first. The question of whether to leave their partner is felt from a loss perspective. Meaning, they fear the loss of emotion. The horse exits into the horse circle first to find out what emotions will help the situation. When, and if, this doesn't work, their rider will progress along the rider circle in search of a problem. They will be more likely to fall into the rider vortices as they are not an expert in this area but less likely to stay. If they can calm their horse in its vortex enough, this will assist them in navigating the rider part of the circle (and not fall into rider vortices) more quickly and efficiently to reach the acceptance point. The Immatures will reactive dramatically to the problem and spend a lot of time in the horse and body vortices. The mature Type 3's will do all of this quicker and with less drama even if their horse is riled.

The type 4 immature journey around the circle parallels the Type 1 except they spend more wasted time and energy (least efficient) in the horse vortex, which are harder to get out of. They will fall into the rider vortices as they are not experts in this area and will also exit quickly as they will give up easy. They will choose to waste time in the horse's vortices as they explore all of these in search of the solution to the problem. They also will attempt to deny the existence of the rider and its approach as they believe the horse has all the answers, further reducing efficiency.

The Type 4 mature, however, will proceed much like the Type 1 mature but in the realm of the horse and its pitfalls. Their horse wouldn't have gotten so riled or reactive in the first place about the problem and will be better able to be managed while their rider navigates the outer circle. They will sense whether the feelings for their partner are strong enough to overcome any other reason for leaving. If there are no feelings, then they leave. They can reach the acceptance point quicker with less lost time and energy than the immature. Also they will be less likely to fall into the horse vortices.

Thus, the Level 1 integrations have an advantage over the un-integrated. Similarly, the Level 2 Integrations are less likely to have their horses exit into the horse circle and get lost in its vortices. Also their riders have the ability to navigate the rider circle more quickly and efficiently with less loss of time and energy. Their riders will also be less likely to exit into the rider vortices and will spend less time there. And more importantly, the next time a problem is encountered, or even the same one, they will be able to stay on the outer circle and avoid it.

The Centaurs will be the most efficient of all of the aforementioned as their horse/rider is strong and integrated. They will encounter the problem with more energy available to deal with it in the first place and their horse will exit quickly from the horse circle after assessing all emotional feelings for staying. It will then continue with the horses as an ally. Their rider will exit into the rider circle after assessing all practical reasons for staying, but will quickly navigate it successfully to the acceptance point, also as an ally. Thus fewer angst, needs or frustrations arise to begin with but the ones that do will be dealt with efficiently (less time and energy wasting, less stressful) as they travel back to the outer circle quickly reaching the acceptance point. They are very well acquainted with the acceptance point as they spend much of their time there. They are an expert in this region because their horse and rider are strong experts in each of their realms. Their rider becomes strong by acquiring powerful knowledge about the universe and developing discipline to achieve its goals. Their horse becomes strong by developing the maximum productive use of its powerful feelings and emotions to achieve its goals. Their body is strong as it is energetic from efficient use of its instincts as aided by the horse and rider.

So we have learned about the nature of the horse and the nature of the rider and the nature of the conflict between them and how they handle conflicts with the universe. We have also seen how the various Types figure into this. Now let's look at the other side of the coin. A calm horse is easier to work with and strengthen as it is not fearful. How do we go about calming the horse and thus calming the rider and thus calm some of the conflicts with the universe.

CHAPTER THREE

Nothing too good or too
Bad lasts too long

How do we calm the horse? First, it will calm down by itself if the rider lets it. Stop the rider from antagonizing the horse. Take care of the horse's fundamental needs so it can be healthy. This concept is acceptable to the horse, who is also listening to this and understands this is a way for him to communicate with the rider. Though, the horse can also get itself worked up over a problem and a strong rider can help calm the horse down by using the reins and discipline to remind the horse that the rider is strong enough to solve a problem without the horse getting anxious.

As mentioned, two common types of problems in humans involve the rider agitating the horse and the horse agitating the rider. If the rider stops agitating the horse it will calm down by itself and vice versa. This accounts for a good percentage of human problems. This is the first step to become a "Level 1 integration". Though, these two problems are intertwined. Each can assist in calming down the other. If the rider is calm, the horse will most likely be calm.....But this requires communication between horse and rider. They have to learn how to calm each other and when to give the other the lead.

Sometimes this is done instinctively. When you are savoring a delicious taste, people often close their eyes. Eyes are the primary way the rider interfaces with the world. (The horse prefers the senses of smell and touch.) This is also why we close our eyes when we meditate or during love making. The rider is deprived of his main avenue of interpreting the world. He thus becomes inactive, allowing the horse to fully concentrate and fully express its opinion of the flavor or experience. This enhances appreciation of the event. This concept can be employed in a lot of different ways. Communication is easier and more easily understood between a calm rider and calm horse.

When the rider talks verbally (out loud) to the horse directly, with no one else around, the horse will listen better than to rider thoughts. The horse trusts the rider's spoken words more than rider thoughts. So if you want to get through to your horse, talk verbally to it even if it seems silly. Rider types often find this idea silly because it seems to them as if it shouldn't be necessary to deal with the horse this way. Similarly, the rider should also allow the horse to verbally speak. The rider should say, out loud, "I love X". X being anything. (Though rider's don't like using the word "love"). This allows the horse an opinion, and allows the rider to know how much the horse likes it, and how it responds to it. Usually Type 1's and 2's don't often do this. A lot depends on which of the four personality Types you are to start with and how integrated they are, and how agitated the horse/rider system is to begin with.

One way the rider agitates the horse (common in Type 2) is with "what if" problems. Too much time spent on non-essential musings of possible detrimental outcomes is exhausting. It is important to "know" which knowledge is important. There are things we "suspect" to be true. There are things we 'believe" to be true. And then there are things we "know" to be true. The rider calms through a maturation process that emphasizes knowledge. And by that I don't mean learning Physics. It wants to know the rules of its universe. This allows it to fulfill its function. This also allows it to control the horse more. It's just a matter of how much control and how much this upsets your horse. The interesting part of this is, if the rider is "upset" by not having its desire met, you can usually still get to sleep at night. But if the horse is "upset" with a problem you usually don't get to sleep. Here are some ways to calm your horse and rider.

Your horse loves unity (the rider likes being alone) and being with the herd or group. It feels most comfortable when surrounded by like thinking individuals. Think of a sporting event where there are people with a common cause, with their team winning. Some fans dress up in ritualistic costumes to show support. There are fight songs where everybody knows the words. This assists in building bonds which is the whole point, all supporting a common cause. All connected. All unified. Political parties, musical groups, the military, and religions also utilize this idea. I will talk about this later.

Your horse responds to consistency which can calm it. Variability heightens the riders need to dominate. The horse also needs consistency from the rider in how he handles things. This develops trust between them. Trust is critical to a calm horse. Mature riders realize this calms the horse. That's why the experimenters in the marshmallow study had to appear to be trustworthy "scientists" so the test would be accepted as valid. If they weren't, the whole study would change.

Your horse responds to noise and constant commotion. Silence or quiet is a welcome respite from the incessant pounding of noise in our everyday clamorous lives. We seem to accept this as a part of life but to the horse it can be draining without our ever realizing it. We, as riders, just accept this as a necessary evil. But noise requires a response from the horse in case it may signal danger. We evolved in a time when we were once prey and more fearful. Prey have to be vigilant and hence fearful, a lot of the time. We still carry this with us, even now, though it is not necessary anymore. Quiet from noise can be calming all by itself.

Your horse responds to repetition, things that happen over and over the same way. It relaxes and lessens the riders need to control the horse. One of the most fundamental and soothing things a human being can experience is rocking or swinging. Its reaches go back to our childhood when as babies we were calmed this way. Get a swing or rocker and when you feel agitated, try it, and feel its therapeutic qualities. And give it time, allow a period of time for it to have effect. Time is perhaps the most calming on a horse also. We never give the horse enough time to be a horse.

Your horse responds to notions of love, freedom, and peace. Feelings. These are its language and how to communicate with it. It does not respond well to things opposing these, which is the world of the rider.

Your rider responds to meditation. This is having the rider calm down so the horse can calm down. The concentration on anything, especially with closed eyes, and the concomitant lack of focus, prevents the rider from being able to do many things at once. There is a Zen saying. "When you are washing the dishes, wash the dishes", do nothing else, think nothing else. Don't be thinking what else you'd rather be doing. Do one thing. Do it well. Then move on. Stay in the now. Good or bad. Meditation can foster this skill. Meditation is a repetitious concentration on something or nothing. Music can achieve the same state. This is also why reading a book in bed is a good way to get to sleep. It relaxes the riders need for control as the rider realizes it is only a book and doesn't require the rider to act.

Your rider responds to the body and vice versa. If the physical sensation is great enough, the rider relaxes and calms, like a warm bath, delicious food, or sex. All of these things emphasize the body and don't require the rider's opinion or input. Emphasize the times when the rider isn't needed. He is overworked as it is. There are more times like this than you think as the rider is overused in our culture. He appreciates a rest as well. This draws distinctions between horse and rider which benefits them both and allows each a chance to input.

Your rider responds to nature. Natural settings instinctively calm the rider. The rider sees less of a need to control here and allows the horse to be guided rather than controlled. This could take the form of a walk by a lake or river. Ask yourself which of these you find more appealing. A lake is calmer.

But some prefer the running water to approximate their temperament.

I was once at a botanical garden and I went from a jungle to a Zen garden. The jungle was wild, diversified, messy, disorganized, and teeming with biological diversity, very high energy. Very horsey.

Then I went to a Zen garden which was peaceful and tranquil. It was low energy and rider orientated with its attention to detail and intrinsic neatness. If one is in an agitated state, the Zen garden is more soothing. If one were in a higher energy state, a good mood, the jungle would be more desirable.

Physical exercise of the body can calm or distract your rider. The body can use the body's energy to perform a physical act and this takes the attention off the rider/horse. You can combine this with nature's therapeutic effect and take a hike. Exercise just for exercises' sake is not appealing to the horse but if you can use exercise as a by-product, like a hike, then the effects are enhanced, more rewarding and most likely to be repeated. This is a requirement for the relaxation to be effective as it has repetition built in which also enhances the product.

The horse-rider system talked about so far basically involves the horse and rider but it is actually a more complex system. The advanced model includes a horse, rider and body as an interacting system. This system can be described schematically with the poles of a triangle representing the horse, rider, and body.

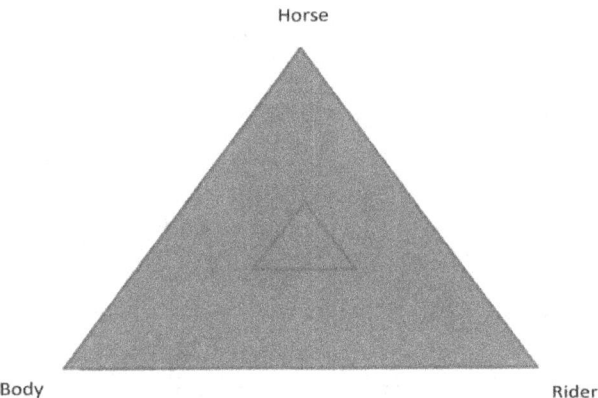

I will talk a bit more about this advanced version later so as not to get confusing now. But since the body is part of the system that needs/assists calming, I will mention it briefly here.

The horse, rider, body system can be represented by a triangle with each member at a pole. When this 3 part system (horse, rider, body) moves toward a pole of the triangle, the other forces diminish as well and not necessarily in proportion. When the body gets attention, like sex, the system goes away from the rider and horse. If you have emotional sex, it goes further from the rider and body. You can also have just sex, very far from horse and rider.

Similarly if the body is tired, the horse and rider has less energy. The rider may want to do something but the horse and body are not on board. You have to get the body on board to start the process, i.e. rest up, then you have to get the horse on board by finding something that motivates it. For example, you might want to condition an exercise routine. Both horse and rider have excuses not to participate. The rider uses discipline to get off the couch and the horse and body follow, provided they offered a carrot.

Similarly, you might use the body's energy, to say, fight illness, then you get the rider on board by using knowledge of the illness to fight it. Then you energize the horse and body. This builds the attitude that you can conquer it and a desire to conquer it. It develops a passion to get well to heal the body. This develops the "go get 'em" attitude that will help to overcome the illness. Then you "enter the zone". Then you have one of the most powerful weapons in the universe. Harmonize the three elements and miracles occur. A Centaur can accomplish this.

Though, sometimes the rider and horse gang up on the body (we are going to diet if you like it or not), and sometimes the horse and body gang up on the rider(we are going to the amusement park whether you like it or not), showing the nature of the shifting alliances and how they learn to work with each other... or choose to not work with each other.

Perhaps most important to the calming and learning of your horse is classical conditioning. This reinforces any learning. I believe that most of whatever got conditioned in the average person's life can be counter conditioned. It just takes time, though there are some smudges that can't be erased, even given time. But the chances of successfully being able to do this depend on what Type you are to begin with and what Level of Integration you have achieved. If you are Integrated to begin with, the chances of dealing successfully with trauma are enhanced. If you have experienced a traumatic incident while un-integrated, (typical in Type1's), it may be useful to integrate first, and then deal with the problem, if you haven't had any success in dealing with it in the first place. The more integrated you are, the easier it is to change your perspective, and to deal effectively with past hurts. Then classical conditioning can help the horse to re-learn differently.

The horse responds like a three year old child. Remember the story at Lake Powell, repetition is how the horse learns, and it creates smudges to help. Smudges can positive or negative. A positive smudge, or investing positive energy, can be followed by another positive smudge giving rise to a positive feeling that gives rise to a positive mood that gives rise to a positive temperament. The idea is to then classically condition this till it becomes a habit and way of life. This whole process instills energy into the system instead of sapping it. Thus it spirals upward. As a practical example of this, there is an expression, "Actions speak louder than words." That's because actions create bigger smudges than words. Actions are the realm of the horse while words are the realm of the rider.

Energy is also a key feature here. The ideas presented here are meant to more efficiently use the energy available in any Type. A lot of people just don't have the energy to live life so they basically give up. But if your rider is calmed, the horse then can become energized to provide the emotions and feelings to deal with the universe. The more energy you have, the easier it is to deal with the changes that constantly occur.

The change from one initial condition to another occurs over a time span. I refer to this as delta T, relating to the time span (degree of change) over which an event occurs. The faster delta T occurs, the harder it is to deal with it. It takes more energy and integration to deal with rapid changes. The balanced horse/rider system has more energy to deal with delta T. In today's world, the rider excels at this, at the expense of the horse. We try to cram more and more into our lives (quantity) at the expense of quality. This makes it harder to cope and harder to integrate and thus harder to calm the horse and rider.

Distraction works wonders on your horse. If you are stuck in a vortex, try just doing anything else. This also works on the rider if he is stuck in analysis paralysis. Try just doing something different. Learn to know when to do this before you waste too much energy swirling in a vortex. Learning when to just walk away for a moment can be quite the skill to learn.

The known or the familiar calms your horse and thus calms your rider. The novel or new is the rider's domain and causes it to become alert, controlling and dominating. When you go to a restaurant, do you pick the same dish you had before that you liked so much, or do you try a new dish? Depends on your temperament, some say, but what they decide to do, depends on whether the horse or rider is in charge at that moment. The known calms the horse, as the rider isn't needed in this venue, so the horse can produce a memory of how good that meal tasted last time or of a favorite comfortable pair of pants or shoes.

You can calm your horse by knowing what causes it pain. Your horse learns by emotional pain. It stores or remembers emotional smudges, both good and bad. This creates something like a battery, an energy source, that is left behind after an experience, but the horse can draw on it later. It creates a "connection". In times of stress, it can be called upon. It is like money in the bank, providing security in times of scarcity. Batteries can be positively charged or negatively charged. A positively charged battery could like a fond memory of a romantic vacation to Mexico. When you think about it you gain energy.

Likewise there are negatively charged batteries that sap your available energy when thought about. We all have lots of these in our past. The negatively charged ones are called baggage. The trick is to discharge the negatively charged ones so they lose their charge, by understanding why they are so negative to the horse and working with the horse to diffuse them. One tries to at least balance the negatively charged ones with the positively charged ones.

Your horse has no sense of time so these smudges can last a long time and sometime morph into something else almost unrecognizable. Horse personal growth involves emotional pain or pleasure. But emotional pain is often fixated on and its healing message is often lost or ignored. Thus we have to repeat it unnecessarily. The idea here is to be non-reactive to emotional pain in a certain way. In the physical body, when there is physical pain due to, say a wound, there is pain to notify us to seek a doctor. The goal isn't to just remove the pain but fix what is causing it. We don't ignore the pain or we might die, so physical pain is good in the bigger picture.

Likewise emotional pain is good but most people don't view it this way. (There is no gift without a problem and no problem without a gift.) But with emotional pain we feel the pain and concentrate so much on it and removing it, that we miss the fact that there is something else that needs our attention. The idea is not to overreact to the emotional pain but rather treat the emotional wound. Remove the ego from the emotional pain. I often phrase it this way, as an example. Once you get angry, you've lost. If you deal with the emotional wound you don't get distracted by anger which is only an indicator of something else.

Naturally the four Types react to this differently. Type 1's don't really like to acknowledge emotional pain (or emotional pleasure for that matter) by attempting to ignore it. Type 2's acknowledge it and deal with it somewhat effectively but usually concentrate on the emotional pain more than the cause. Type 3's over react to the emotional pain and also fail to address the real issue. Type 4's dwell on the emotional pain and totally ignore the cause. Naturally the mature versions of the Types deal with the subject differently. I think you can see how by now. If not, here is an example.

In my earlier book, two characters were talking. One was a nerd named Wendell (immature Type 1) who got picked on in school. He was talking to Father John (mature Type 3) about how people use to call him names and it how it hurt. Father John says, "If I were to call you a couch would you get upset?" "No", answers Wendell. Father John replies, "Right, because you aren't one. So the label doesn't apply. If I was to call you an asshole would you get upset?" "Yes." Replies Wendell. Father John then tells him "Why?, does the label apply?" "No." responds Wendell. "Well then don't get upset. You just reacted because you're ego got involved." A reactive immature horse will respond like this where a mature one would not. The ability to rise above things requires a calm horse and calm rider working together to change the perspective of each.

Being non-reactive (the realm of the Centaur) can be very helpful. Nature actually has a built in mechanism to help with this. Imagine a mother who just was in a car accident with her infant who was badly injured. She doesn't feel emotional pain right there because she has to deal with the crisis first. She detaches in order to save the infant. The detachment is for the greater good, very much like shock works in the physical body. She can detach from the emotional pain to save her infant, so why not detach In lesser situations and deal with the emotional pain? This is a skill that can be learned.

It is interesting that emotional pain has no organ in the physical body to produce it, like a heart attack has the heart organ. It is interesting to ask people, if they had the choice, which would they choose to experience, emotional pain or physical pain. Then ask them if which is easier to detach from. We can detach to help another human or we can detach to heal. But we can't do what's in our best interest until we learn how to change how we feel without pain determining results. We need to learn how to change how we feel in order to change how we think and vice versa. And then learn when to do each gracefully. A Centaur does this routinely.

So, it is possible to change sponsoring thoughts without pain influencing results. (A sponsoring thought is a powerful fundamental thought that gives rise to our other thoughts, like the root thought.) Then we aren't slaves to our emotions. We change our rational minds all the time without pain. We used to believe that we knew gravity because of what Newton taught us. Then Einstein comes along and says no, Newton was wrong, this is how it really is. We say "ah ha" and change without emotional pain.

So let's step back and review what we have learned about the horse and rider so far.

Learning about the horse and the rider was step 1 in becoming a Centaur. This was talked about in the introduction and Chapter 1. Chapter 2 was about conflicts between the horse and rider. Much of Chapter 3 was concerned with ways to calm the rider which calms the horse which calms the rider. That was step 2 to becoming a Centaur. Step 3, in the next Chapter, is about becoming mature enough to see beyond your own perspective, be it horse "or" rider or horse "and" rider. But to be able to do this you need to have both the horse and rider calm. So that was what Chapter 3 was about. But, to be able to mature enough to continue, to be able to get out of your own way, to go beyond your own perspective gracefully, is explored in the next Chapter.

CHAPTER FOUR

Letting go changes everything
Because letting go changes nothing

So, we have seen the horse in some of its manifestations and the rider in some of its manifestations. We have also seen how they interact and inter-react, pro and con. Now we look at the pair as they mature by changing perspectives. And how the integrated whole is many times greater than the sum of its parts.

It probably seems evident by now what happens when the parts relate and don't relate. Also, how the benefits of dealing with a calm horse and rider make the Integration process easier. The next step is to integrate the horse and rider by learning how to change perspective. Keep in mind the horse and rider find it Equally hard to detach from their own perspectives. Though the horse finds it as easy to detach from rider type problems as the rider finds it to detach from horse type problems. Thus, the successful and agreeable integration of these two separate, strong, and unique viewpoints is a challenge. But if you can master this feat, the universe will reward you. Your universe will then teach you at an accelerated rate when you willing and capable of paying attention.

The primary benefit of harmonious integration (a Centaur) is a human that is non-judgmental, non-reactive, not attached to a particular outcome, balanced, in harmony, peaceful, more intuitive, calm and energized to deal with the universe and its trials and tribulations. Thus, happy. I don't mean this as the feeling people get when eating ice cream. It is much deeper and more comprehensive than that. Whenever an individual has available calm, controlled energy I define this state as happiness, much like the state we described when one is "in the zone". This state is restful and peaceful and conducive to healing. Think about when you have been happy, isn't there always a feeling of available calm energy. The reason there is available energy is because the horse and rider are in balance. The rider can direct the energy. If we have more energy, we can tolerate change better. Too little and we don't want change. This available calm energy also facilitates acceptance and co-operation. (This type of calm energy also biochemically reduces negative feelings and contrasts with the wild uncontrolled energy of fear or anxiety).

I believe the natural state of a balanced and mature human being is happy. This sounds almost silly to some because it sounds like a Polly-Anna viewpoint. One can't be happy that much. This shows how out of whack most people are. They can't even conceive of the notion of being happy for an extended period of time. Sad state of affairs.

This matured combination of horse and rider, this combined version, doesn't need or want to judge, as the ego is calm. Like your immune system, just patiently waiting and ready if a disease strikes. It doesn't get offended, as there is no reason to. It is non-reactive. It is detached and freed from petty small picture stuff. It doesn't react to the small stuff as most human stuff is small. It rises above it all, flowing over the rocks in the river rather than getting bounced to and fro and hitting the rocks like at low flows of a river, or low energy. The Centaur realizes there is, like floods and droughts, nothing too good or too bad that lasts very long anyway. This matured horse and rider persona, allows for perspective changes to happen easier. This idea is sometimes talked about in Zen.

There is a story in my first book about a Zen master talking with his student about dualistic thinking. The master says "You, with your dualistic thinking. You think a door can only be open or closed. But there is a third choice, it can be half open. Most of life occurs between these poles of yours." There are no poles anyway. There are no opposites, only differences. And there does not have to be opposition between differences. The rider manufactures these supposed opposites to support its agenda.

Using this principle we can actually change reality. Our perception or feelings of reality determines reality to a large extent. We are literally gods that can change our universe if we wish. We have the ability to change our perception. And it is a lot easier to change perception if are integrated with available calm energy. The ugly can be made beautiful by changing perception, and vice versa. The beautiful water lily has its roots in mud. Nature doesn't use the energy it has to react. It uses the energy to create.

So changing perception is easier to do when you have available energy. This is where Zen comes in. Actually, there are a lot of ways to change perception (some based on horse and some based on rider) but I choose Zen here because it seems to allow changing perception to a very large degree, but it is rider based, so it will have the largest effect on Types 1 or2.

This is the way a rider creates a smudge through the "Ah ha" moment. This allows you to be able to change perception to the degree that it can change your paradigms and thus personality structure. (All of the four basic personality Types will do this differently and at various rates of success.) Seems a tall order but it can be done. Once you have a mature horse and rider it can expand the horizons of the universe and the foundations of your world will change, as it was meant to be. The ability to change perception allows us to evolve, mature and grow up to become a Centaur.

As an example of this ability to change perception from the rider's view, to live outside the box, I reference a koan that I wrote about in my first book. A koan, in Zen, is a question that is impossible to answer. Its goal is to humble the rider and show its limitations so it doesn't become a dictator with its power, to show the advantages of non-rational thinking (not irrational which is something quite different).

I chose the koan, "We know the sound of two hands clapping, what is the sound of one hand clapping?" In my first attempt to answer it, (I should say, respond to it as there is no answer) I held up one hand and snapped my fingers. Thus, one hand clapping. I was a smart ass back then. Anyway, it was way too rational an answer. After more soul searching I came up with a different response. When asked the question, "What is the sound of one hand clapping?" I responded by sitting still and saying nothing, demonstrating the sound of one hand clapping. Thus, responding without words which distort reality. Closer, but I still had to go deeper into the realm of the horse. My final response to the question of "What is the sound of one hand clapping?" involves a non-rational answer that borders on art.

Art is non-rational. I find it amusing when I am staring at a painting and a person asks me, "What do you think of that painting?" The question should be, "What do you feel about that painting?" Apples and oranges. Horse and rider. So when I tell you my response please attempt to view it in this manner, from the horse perspective and not the rider. Also it took me a year to come up with the response so it will take a lot of thought to fully understand what I mean when I tell you it.

My response was, "Tires floating in the air are perfectly acceptable." What I was trying to convey in a short version is that if you can accept the impossible (tires floating in the air) than how difficult is it to accept the possible? Once you can do this you can accept anything. What is left? This is a very powerful tool to deal with the universe.

Another example of this on a different plane is a scene between a Zen master and his advanced student sitting in a field on a hot summer day. The master says, "Is there snow here?" The student wisely responds, "Yes. There is no snow today". This indicates the range of all possibilities. No snow is included in the possibilities. If you have snow you must have no snow as well. Remember both are always present, only a matter of time which doesn't really exist anyway, except to the rider.

These are examples of how the rider can change its perception, but the horse can change its perception too, but it leaves more of a smudge than the riders "Ah ha" moments. And often times it involves fear.

Emotionally, fear makes the picture smaller. When you are afraid you don't think about finishing college or what you will be when you grow up. You zoom down to the smaller picture. The zoom is controlled by the horse/body. When this is the focus, all else pales. And you cannot change perception until you decrease pressure or stress on the horse, i.e., the things that made it fearful. And this procedure can also be positive in nature. Love can change perception too, that is horse.

This ability to change perceptions allows the shift from small picture to BIG picture and vice versa, to extricate ourselves from the mundane to the spiritual. We go from reacting to it all to an acceptance of what it all is. We can detach from the petty. We can accept what is. The universe becomes perfect as it is. Our needs and wants adjust accordingly. Suddenly we don't need a Ferrari to be happy. We don't need to kill our boss to be happy.

We can evolve from the world of needs, wants and possessions that posse us. We begin life believing that the "be and end all" is fulfilling needs. Having is everything. Then we discover that having is not so great a thing as wanting. Then wants consume us. The horse is running rampant. When we mature we learn less can be more. That more is not the answer. We learn discipline and control the horse. But if we use to much we become unhappy for other reasons. The seesaw teeters constantly back and forth, through the balance point for a second, and then on to the other extreme.

Hopefully the seesaw settles down. This is when there is harmony between horse and rider, at the balance point, the point of maximum diversity. Acceptance occurs at the maximum of each swing. Acceptance means releasing the energy that you have been pushing toward something. The sooner you accept, the sooner the seesaw goes back towards the balance point. This is maturity. This is how we each mature. Of course it is done differently depending on which of the four personality Types you are.

Perhaps the biggest feature of a mature horse and rider is an understanding of the concepts of acceptance (the importance of which was seen in the Circle Figure) and non-reactiveness. These are two key assets of the Centaur. To know that true victory sometimes means accepting surrender, and to not react is a true test of really listening. This requires a trust and understanding between horse and rider. But if you can do this with your horse and rider, you can do it with everything else in your life, even tires.

A trust can develop between horse and rider. This trust is essential as it allows the horse to relax or become non- reactive to stresses or fears. There can be a partial maturity when one matures but not the other, but when they both mature, then the beauty blossoms. The horse generally cannot mature before the rider. The rider matures first and waits for the horse to arrive somewhat later. This is because our culture spends a lot of time attempting to mature the rider as it is viewed as the most important component. The horse is neglected. It is the rider that needs to learn how to make a buck, get a house, to advance in the company, to get to the moon, to solve problems that matter, everything else is unimportant.

The bottom line is that the rider matures through knowledge and the horse matures through trust. Three year old kids have nightmares about monsters because the rider hasn't developed to the point that the monsters can be controlled or even understood. The monsters have not yet been put into a rider trustworthy "box".

But the rider is somewhat limited by the box. As I said, I was trained as a classical scientist to explore all the wonderful beauty inside the box. But when studying Zen it hit me how rationality is limited. In Zen they use koans routinely to explore outside the box, also a very beautiful and wondrous place.

Does "inside the box" thinking answer all problems? It can't. For instance, which came first the chicken "or" the egg? Well to get a chicken you need an egg and to get an egg you need a chicken. Age old question. Well I can answer it. Not using rational thought but rather a more sophisticated form of rationality found outside the box. Not irrational thought but non-rational thought. The answer is, the chicken is the egg. They are the same thing. Again notice the influence of "or" versus "and".

What we humans tend to do is take unity and split it into component parts to understand it. Then we immediately forgot we have done so and spend the rest of our lives trying to harmonize something we artificially split apart. All the time wondering why it doesn't make sense. The reason I mention this is because this fractal idea of starting with unity, then splitting from it, and then coming back together is all over, even with horse and rider, even with male and female. It is fractal.

It has been said men are from Mars and women are from Venus. Thus artificially drawing them worlds apart when in actuality they are closer than the atoms they are both made of. If men are from Mars and women from Venus, then Centaurs are from Earth, which is right between Mars and Venus. There is some male in females and some female in males. Males and females are just like the chicken and the egg. When this is truly understood, a man can truly understand how a woman thinks and feels, and vice versa. One of the most important parts of this book is to demonstrate that everything in the universe is like this. The Centaur understands this implicitly. We need to view the universe in a non- dualistic way.

I have discussed the unifying of the horse and rider but first we separated them to understand the components isolated. Horse and rider are actually opposite ends of the same stick. Got how it works? .... Good and bad (supposed opposites) are also different ends of the same stick. There are no opposites unless we make it so. There are only differences in the universe and they don't have to be opposing. Nothing is ever good or bad but shades of both. A practical example of this principle is that there is no problem without a gift and no gift without a problem.

A story told long ago that exemplifies this idea concerns a conversation between a dog and a wolf. A dog was quietly munching on a steak bone outside a cabin in the woods. He was chained to a post just outside the cabin door. Up walks a wolf and sits down beside him. The wolf says, "Boy, are you lucky. You get a guaranteed meal every day, you have a master that loves you and cares for you. You don't have to worry about dying in the wilderness fighting to survive. You don't have to survive the cold winter". The dog just sat there listening to the wolf and nodding to what he was saying. Finally, he looks the wolf straight in the eye and says, "Everything you said is true and more. But I would trade it all of it to get rid of this chain and live free like you. Free to go wherever you want when you want. You are the lucky one and don't even know it." The wolf thought about this for a while and finally said, "Thank you so much" and turned and left. Can you see horse and rider in this story?

Which reminders me of another story with a similar meaning. It is a famous Zen story about a Zen master who owned a horse ranch (Thank God it was a horse ranch). I leave it to you to decide if horses are good or bad.

The ranch was going into foreclosure because the mortgage couldn't be paid. The son of the master comes running in one day screaming," I found a herd of wild horses. We can sell them and save the ranch. Isn't that great? All is good." The Zen master says, "We'll see."

The next day his son comes hobbling in after he fell off a horse trying to break it, but instead, nearly killed himself and broke his leg. He screams, "Those horses are terrible. They nearly killed me. They are really a curse. All is bad." The Zen master says. "We'll see."

The next day the General of the Army rides in and tries to conscript the son. But he can't take him because he has a broken leg. The son says, "Those horses really are a blessing. All is good." The Zen master says, We'll see." .... I think you get the message. Nothing too good or too bad lasts too long. Dualistic thinking (seeing opposite ends of the same stick as two separate sticks) is just a rider generalization. And all generalizations are to some degree wrong, including the one I just made.

As another practical example of a dualistic system, take the immune system. Is it good or bad? Most say it's good. But what if you have an autoimmune disease? (That's when the immune system attacks its own body) Then it's bad. But when it's calm the immune system is wonderful. It defends the body. But if it is agitated or abused it can become your worst nightmare. The idea is know it and keep it calm. Similarly, the ego in the psyche has the job of defending and protecting the psyche. But if it is agitated or inflamed it can injure the psyche. The idea is to know it and keep it calm. Similarly, on a larger scale, prejudice helps defend the culture from attack. It is also a defense mechanism. All are defense mechanisms that can become "offensive" if not calmed. All are acting the same way, either this or that.

But the world is not black or white. (Doors do not have to be only open or closed ...there is a third state, it can be half opened). It is not even shades of gray. It is not even shades of all colors. It is not even only the entire electromagnetic spectrum. This is the broader perspective provided by the Centaur.

One of the goals of this book is to develop a way to change the way you think by changing how you feel, and also to change how you feel by changing how you think, by using an Integrated horse And rider to decide when to do each. This is the goal of using horse and rider theory, to learn balance and gain maturity. How and when should your horse decide what to do and how and when should your rider decide what to do? And to have the ability to know when to implement each or both. Which should you choose to implement your best interest? The curious thing is that it always requires both acting in concert to get the fullest picture. And even then will it always turn out right? ..."We'll see."

So, in Zen, there is an emphasis on the rider and changing its perception, and hence, perspective of the rational world. After all, it is easier to civilize the rider than the horse. All civilization is really just the rise of the rider at the expense of the horse. All the rules, laws, structure, were invented by the rider to protect itself from other uncontrolled horses. It is easier for the rider to understand the horse than the other way around, as it should be easier for a civilized man to understand an undeveloped man than an undeveloped man to understand a civilized man. However, horse and rider theory is not about an evolution of an apple into an orange. The rider didn't use to be a horse.

As far as the genetic evolution of horse and rider is concerned, the horse came first. The horse is part of the limbic system and that evolved first. It took a long time to develop the pre-frontal -cortex to allow the rider to be born. It is the last part of the brain to evolve. It is the thin veneer of the brain, the tip of the iceberg, the frosting on the cake. Thus, often the most primitive part of the brain is accessed first to deal with reality, with the slower more accurate part accessed second.

Civilization has only been around for about 5,000 years, the riders created world, but the horse has been around for millions. It's a wonder the rider has any control at all. But the horse doesn't mature as fast as the rider and takes even longer if without a strong rider. But, does maturity have to take a long time? Yes, without a strong rider. No, if you have a strong rider. All of the personal stories I mentioned earlier, like whether to jump, whether to eat marshmallows, whether to overdo alcohol, were a function of this. All were designed to lead us to Centaur-hood.

So we have this Centaur "being" that is a merging of the two. It now has abilities that neither one had to begin with. It has emergent properties. It is non-judgmental, non-reactive, a calm ego and the Centaur can feel empathy. A higher order feeling that the horse couldn't possess. Sympathy is when one can understand (rider) what it feels like to be in another's shoes. Empathy is when you actually feel (horse) it. The mature rider can say, if that was me I would feel this way. Immature horses don't care if the deer on the other side of the fence just got shot. The immature rider doesn't care if he has to steal another kid's blocks to build his tower higher. But empathy is a combination of horse and rider. The Centaur can feel another person's pain. It is also acutely aware of the separate roles of the horse, rider and body and how each feels.

As I have mentioned before, another more advanced form of the horse rider model theory is when the physical body is added to the system. Then the two dimensional system becomes three dimensional. It can be described by a triangle with three poles of rider, horse, and body. The balance point is now at the center of the triangle. Around it forms a zone of triangular phase space where we spend most of our lives. What we now see is the true form of integration. The seesaw doesn't swing just between two poles, but three. At each pole is the maximum energy, or expression, of the components of the system.

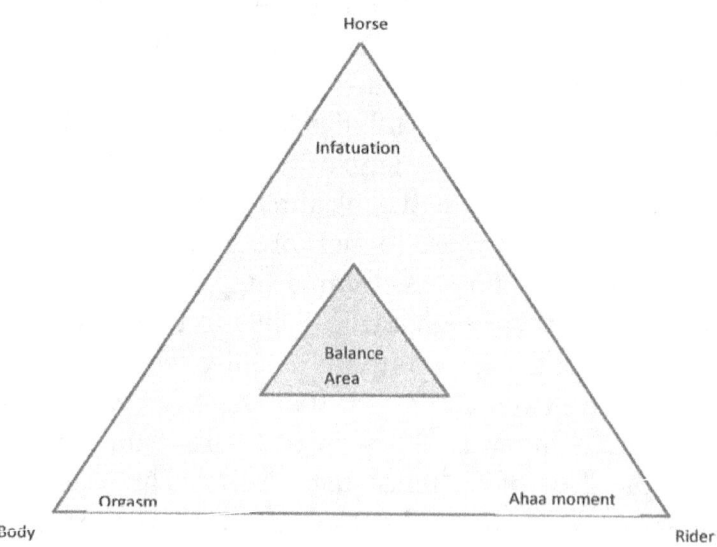

At the rider pole, the purest form is the "Ah Ha" moment, almost pure rider. The moment of understanding new knowledge and how it fits in the universe. The rider fully expressed. At the physical pole we see one of the greatest manifestations of the body as the orgasm. The body fully expressed. And at the horse pole we see one of the greatest manifestations as the infatuation experience. The horse fully expressed. These are peak experiences when the system is most out of balance, though quite entertaining. We see, as each pole is nearing, the other two elements recede, not necessarily in proportion. But it takes energy to push toward a pole and thus we don't stay there long. There is also an equal release of energy as the poles are left behind as the energy turns to grief as the system heads back toward the balance point.

There is an area of comfort called the phase space in the center of the triangle where the person is most at home, where he chooses to spend most of his time. It is always in motion. Remember, it is never static as the human condition and the universe seeks to push boundaries. A static system is a broke system. That's not the way the universe was designed to function. There is maximum diversity and the most of each pole at the center point. We are designed to explore the whole triangle but we must use what we have learned to maximize the system, which means finding the balance area. We spend our lives careening over this triangle trying to find the "best" (most temporarily comfortable) spot. But the "best" spot keeps changing.

But the more integrated we are, the stronger we become, as we gain more and more from integration and it becomes easier and easier. As another

emergent property of the integration, we gain
wisdom. This allows us to view other perspectives
and thus broadens our perspective.

Another emergent property of integration is
mature intuition. The rider interprets the messages of
the horse and tests them by trusting them in certain
ways, to get a feel for the horses judgment, to help
decide if a business venture will succeed or not. Some
people are said to "have a knack" for something. Or
they sometime are referred to as "lucky". This is
when horse and rider are in balance and mature.
When matured the horse and rider have more
patience to listen to the more subtle clues that the
universe is chock full of. This is often when miracles
or luck happen.

We tune into unseen frequencies that teach us
things we are now ready and able to learn. We sense
things as well as know them. We know things
without knowing how or why. We become luckier.
The door to the metaphysical is now open. However,
it is not just metaphysical but applied metaphysical as
the rider component merges his knowledge as well.
We can thus grasp concepts that previously made no
sense.

An example of this is the transition in Physics
when we evolved from Classical Newtonian
Mechanics to Quantum Mechanics. Classical
Newtonian Physics was strictly "in the box" stuff,
very straightforward, linear and logical. Then
Quantum Mechanics appeared because we were
ready for it. In Quantum Mechanics, classical rules
made no sense. How does the description of one atom
change the description of another atom on the other

side of the universe instantaneously? How can a cat be dead and alive at the same time? No problem in the quantum world. There aren't just two possible states, there are three. This changed all the laws. It broadened our perspective. Although it didn't really change anything, it's just a different world at the very small scale.

A curious thing about all this, is that Quantum Mechanics is to Newtonian Physics as the horse is to the rider. It's all quite fractal. Quantum Physics is like the horse and the emotions in that it appears chaotic and unfathomable only because it plays by such radically different rules. In Quantum Mechanics just the act of observing an event changes it. Just like recognizing an emotion can change it. The observer is inextricable linked to the observed. Newtonian mechanics is linear, more easily predictable and less chaotic. It is so beautiful how this is all fractal, meaning it occurs everywhere on all scales. It is the very fabric of the universe. And I might mention, it took the greatest minds we had at the time to integrate these two parts of physics together and even that integration is still awkward, like a Level 1 Integration.

So in Chapter 4 we saw the value of learning how to change perspective to assist in becoming a Centaur. This was the third step in becoming a Centaur, how to change your perspective. I came up with a good way to demonstrate this idea in your everyday life and I put it in my first book. There was a scene with a low income, underachieving basketball team who got a chance to play the elite, powerhouse, much better talent, rich team for the Championship. They were standing around before the game, feeling like they didn't have a chance to win when the main character walks up and tells them that they are going to lose if they don't change their perspective. He tells them, "Before you can be great you have to think you are great". It doesn't matter if it is true or not.

Now the rider will naturally balk at this (this is the main reason the process usually stops here) as often it isn't true at first and the rider strongly dislikes buying into something it knows isn't true. But sometimes you do have to fully believe this anyway to get the horse on board. It is a method to break into the circle of something greater. You have to imagine and believe, despite.... Suspend your disbelief. Sometimes this can create a miracle or at least a new branch of Physics.

Another similar approach to putting this idea into action is also in that book I wrote. Two characters were talking about a lone flower growing in a barren desert. One character says to the other, "How can that grow there?" The other character says. "Because it doesn't know it's not supposed to." Again demonstrating how to evolve your horse and rider system by changing perspective, to go beyond your current level of understanding to Integrate a strong horse and rider. An imagination, the horse, helps this transition to occur rather than hindering it.

Step 4 in becoming a Centaur is to implement all these ideas. Learn it, Think it, Act it, Become it. Condition it. To go beyond yourself and evolve. To actually get out of your own way. Before you can become a Centaur sometimes it helps to just behave like one. Break the circle anyway you can. Evolve. Be

Fearless. Don't be the person on their death bed begging for one more chance to do it right.

So we have looked at the horse and rider model to explain and help ourselves but can it also explain relationships with other people and help make them more successful. Yes.

CHAPTER FIVE

It's not about finding the "right"
Mate. But rather, making yourself
The "right" mate.

This Chapter deals with an analysis of male/ female relationships in terms of how one horse/rider system relates to another horse/rider system. When one understands everything that has been said so far, it becomes easy to see that this is the second most important part. The first part is getting your own horse and rider integrated.

I will go into details of the 4 personality Types based on the horse-rider model and how they go together in male/female relationships. Please keep in mind the four Types represent a broad spectrum and do not have black and white (sharp) boundaries.

All of the four Types are attempting to make sense of themselves while attempting to integrate themselves and deal with the universe and its demands. At the same time, we also attempt to integrate others (personal relationships) into our lives. Sometimes these people can have a very different perspective than our own. This is a daunting prospect. Of course, the Type and Integration Level of the participants will have a large impact on how successful this will be.

Let's take a look at how all the Types go together, remembering that the more integrated people will exhibit more of the strength traits of the Type, and contrariwise, the more immature Types will exhibit more of the weaknesses of the Type.

We must first keep in mind the very nature of the rider orientated person will give rise to a very different approach to love, and all its permutations, than that of a horse oriented person. The rider approach to affection, love, and even sex will follow a predictable pattern. Love, affection and sex itself will be short, efficient, classical positions, predictable, nothing kinky, and rather unremarkable. Kisses and hugs will be short, quick and perfunctory as the rider attempts to mimic what it thinks horse behavior consists of. Love is obviously the realm of the horse. Sex is as close to the realm of the horse as the rider likes to get. So often times the rider has to "use" love to get sex and the horse has to "use" sex to get love. The Centaur is a master of both.

Love is the realm of the horse, and the rider usually makes a mockery of it, though of course, the rider will never admit this. Thoughts in the rider head during sex center around "doing it right". That is the most important thing.

Now, the horse orientated person in love is quite different, as it can be very unpredictable. Love making will be long, sensual, expressive, any position goes, and is done with abandon. Kisses and hugs are long and passionate with the rider being left behind. There is only the now and sensual feelings. And no thought about the sensual feelings, just the feelings themselves. Horses like sweet nothings whispered in their ears and touch is a primary means of communication.

Along these lines, there was a book written about the primary ways people love, The Five Love Languages by Gary Chapman. The author listed some of the ways love can be expressed. Two of them consisted of gift giving and service orientated acts. These are the way of the rider lover. And, by now, you can see why. Other ways to express love listed in that book consisted of touch and sweet words. These are the ways of the horsey lover. So one can see how a rider may claim to be "loving" their partner but the partner may not feel loved at all, and vice versa.

As I have mentioned, horses and riders are apples and oranges to each other in all things. Now the people who have matured to "Level 1 Integration" will have some of each of the preceding mentioned characteristics of love. Sometimes one side may show up and sometime the other. Hopefully the other person can make adaptations to meld harmoniously.

At the "Level 2 Integration", love making occurs with little talking and the lovers move as one. Both instinctively knowing exactly what to do and when, to please their partner. There are tight embraces, two bodies in sync, feelings are understood and agreed upon. There is a "giving" of the horse, unlike the taking of the rider. There is no awkwardness or tension, but rather more relaxed. This shared level of communication allows an integration to occur between them so they both "enter the flow". After all, God made us in halves to keep warm in the desert.

The "Level 2 Integration" version of love and love making is what we all seek. It is almost like a Hollywood version, since Hollywood specializes in understanding the horse. It is almost mythical in nature as there aren't many people who can do this, let alone find a partner who can also do it. So we do the best we can.

As I mentioned in the beginning, and it deserves repeating, many people are swept away trying to navigate in a violent emotional storm in their "raft" that has many holes in it (most of them self-created). Tossed upon a stormy sea is scary enough without having to patch holes in the middle of it. Then people attempt to bring people into their raft to assist or save them before they fixed the holes. And the raft then sinks and they curse the universe for the storm. The first part of this book deals with harmonizing your horse and rider. This section deals with harmonizing another horse and rider with yours. Naturally if your horse and rider are integrated beforehand you are a much better partner in a relationship.

Generally an un-integrated horse and rider tries to have a relationship with another horse and rider out of sync and I think you see why I am glad the divorce rate is only 50%. So, the next best thing is to have only one un-integrated (a Level 1 Integration coupled with a horse or rider). This produces better results.

Having two Level 2 integrated people together is rather rare. These are known as soul mates. If you have ever seen a thoroughbred at a horse race they always have a stable mate that calms them down, one that gets along really well with the other. They complement each other. They are like a comfortable pair of pants (shoes) to the other. The purpose of this section is to show how a horse and rider work, and don't work, with another horse and rider in a male female relationship. Let's look at all the various types of horse/rider personalities (Types 1-4) and various levels of integration and see how they all go together.

First, as I said, the more mature of any Type is the more integrated and this will produce more positive qualities (and hence better relationship material) with which to work. The immature versions will have more of the weaknesses and fears and hence, have a tougher time making it work. A mature (broader perspective) version of any Type has a good chance with any Type, though there are better mixes than others.

Let's look at horse Or rider and the immature variety, as they are common. The Type 4 immature can be emotionally needy and/or reactive and overly sensitive. This leads them to be selfish and self-absorbed about fulfilling their needs via a partner.

If you can understand your horse and address its emotional needs, then and only then, can you understand and address the emotional needs of another's horse. A mature version (Level 1 or Level 2 integration) creates deeper feelings from the two horses in sync. This allows them to truly inter-relate. This dance is in tune and is much prized. However, that is not the normal state of affairs, so let's look at two immature horses not in sync.

The pre-described angst and frustration of not being integrated could produce an emotionally reactive, passionate, jealous, unpredictable, horse. If this type of horse (type 4 meets type 4) meets another horse like it, then the relationship will fly together fast and fly apart faster. It will be intense, passionate and short, usually followed by more of the same in a vain attempt to find a way to sail their leaky raft between two hurricanes.

If this Type 4 immature meets any other Type, the results will be the same, though lasting a little longer. Though a Type 4 immature would seldom consider a Type 1 immature as Type 4 immatures are as completely opposite from immature Type 1's as you can get. But if one of the Type 4's can evolve to a Type 3, then there is some hope for a more successful relationship because he/she might be able to assist the other Type 4 to evolve as well. Sometimes evolution can be contagious.

Alternatively if two immature riders (two Type 1's) come together, they will probably come together slower and with less passion but build a friendship that is longer lasting than that of the Type 4's just mentioned. They will be able to co-exist longer. But eventually, the battles for control and dominance will retard this relationship. But if one of the Type 1's can evolve to a Type 2 then there is also hope for a deeper relationship because he/ she could assist the other in evolving.

Sometimes the rider bonds (attraction without a strong emotional component) can be satisfying and sometimes not. They also can drift apart after trials, tribulations and life pressures put a telling toll on this type of bond. The horse's emotional bonds create smudges that last longer than the riders smudges, so one without the other is not as sustainable. This is why the Types 1's prefer Type 2's in relationships. These two Types are often found together for the same reason that Type 3's and Type 4's are often found together.

So how much of each Type is required for a successful relationship? There must be components that satisfy the rider, like a sound, reliable friendship that can be counted on in times of stress and new challenges. There must also be a sense of comfort from the known, like a comfortable pair of pants which satisfies the horse. There must also be a physical connection (the body) that provides the energy component of the relationship that also must fit together. If you have all these in your relationship count yourself lucky. There is then a harmony that each horse, rider, and body can revel in. Then you can do more than just play the notes, but instead make music.

So, we have looked at horse and horse together (Type 4's) and rider and rider (Type 1's) together. How about one of the other types? What would a Type 2 and Type 3 relationship look like? The Type 2 and Type 3's have a better starting point for a successful relationship as they are similarly integrated. This type of relationship usually feels good because we see a lack in ourselves that we see fulfilled in another. This also provides a longer lasting relationship than Type 4 to Type 4 because there is a stronger rider component. Each will enjoy seeing the other express something they are, and aren't, at different times, as they each have some horse and some rider in them. At times a Type 2 can be horsey, and rider-ish at others and his/her Type 3 partner can relate to it.

Differences tend to attract for a short while but similarities go the distance. BUT having both is the ultimate answer. Again, "or" is not as good as "and". Thus 2's and 3's tend to have successful relationships, especially if they evolve to Level 2 integration. (Each evolution to the next highest integration gets easier and less painful and more successful). And as I have said numerous times, balance is the key. Horse and rider should be in balance with the needs of the other horse and rider. If each can be addressed in yourself then each of your partner's needs can be addressed in a similar manner. We treat the needs of our partner just like we treat the needs of our horse. (Curiously enough, we also treat the needs of our pets the same as we treat the needs of our horse.)

It should also be restated that a mature form of any type could be ok with any other type even if the other is immature, depending somewhat on how immature, but it will be more likely to be successful if it is a Type 2 or 3 because there is more shared components. Likewise, without reservation, two mature of the same Types are a desirable combination. Although, the Centaur, being integrated, will exhibit the strengths of all 4 types. It will relate to all of them. It will be the most successful in a relationship, for a lot of reasons.

It can be seen that Type 2 and Type 3 are close in compatible style but it is interesting that Type 2's or Type 3's will probably superficially prefer a Type 1 or Type 4 as the differences attracts them and they like the lack of internal conflict and surety in these Type 1's or 4's. Also they are initially attracted by the confidence that a black and white perspective appears to offer. A Type 2 might be attracted to a Type 1 as a means of solidifying their inconstant nature by choosing a stable "rock" to lean and learn from. Likewise, a type 3 might look to a type 4 to find, deal with, and explore more of their emotional side to come to grips with dealing with it. But long term better mates for them are fellow 2's and 3's. For one thing, the evolution to potential higher maturity has a higher probability with other 2's and 3's. They will probably stagnate with Type 1's or 4's. The Type 3's might get tired of nurse-maiding an immature Type 4 or a Type 2 will probably get tired of the overbearing immature Type 1.

Also, the bonds created by evolving together are very strong. A hallmark of successful relationships is an ability to grow with changes and stay together Because of them. So picking a person who is capable of change or growth (integration) is very important. Type 1's and Type 4's have a greater challenge achieving this if they are immature. Though the more mature ones will know to look for a Type 2 or 3 to help evolve themselves and give the relationship a better chance of success. I should also say Type 1's and 4's can evolve to Level 1 or Level 2 Integration. It just takes longer and is more challenging as the horse and rider have to get acquainted and learn to work together. This first step is the most difficult.

Relationships between Type 1's and 3's as well as relationships between Type 4 and 2's have similar challenges. Though a Type 1 and Type 3 relationship will tend to last longer than a Type 4 and Type 2 as the rider component of the Type 1 can "make" the relationship work even if it doesn't "really" work. The Type 3 will go along with this for a while in the interests of co-operation. The horse can be subjugated but at a cost that eventually has to be paid. The people in the Type 4 and Type 2 relationship will see the flaw earlier but reach a similar conclusion.

So, please note, there is a difference between having a good relationship and making a relationship work. I think everybody "senses" this and some "know" it. This is very similar to your own horse having a good relationship with your own rider, versus your horse and rider "making it work". I hope you can see if have to "make" your horse and rider have a good relationship then you probably are involved in a relationship that you are "making" work. Please don't assume I think that relationships don't require "work", as I do, but the horse "working" with a rider is much more likely to produce a success and is much more efficient.

Now that I have mentioned the spectrum of personality types and the effects of maturity on them, there is another component that I have mentioned in earlier chapters. That is the role of the body in relationships. The body is a source of energy to the horse rider system. Every person is born with a certain level of energy and depending on the level of Integration, this available energy level can be used to deal with the universe and its demands. This energy level comes out in the personality of each person, and in relationships it helps to have it matched.

The energy level of each horse rider system will tell you things such as how active a person is, or what he/she is capable of doing and how they use it to deal with the universe's demands. Also high energy types tend to use their available energy to cover up a lot of problems the same way Hollywood uses special effects to cover up a weak plot.

Bullies also use energy to cover weaknesses/insecurities. High energy adds a dimension to any Type, but it must be filtered through maturity to be energy efficient as high energy can be draining in a relationship if not used properly.

Energy can be used as power as well. In Type 1 males, the high energy (Alphas) immatures can become overbearing and in females, Type 4, the high energy immatures can manifest as "high maintenance". Lower energy Types are quieter and less demanding and manifest as Betas. Culturally high energy is prized by our rider orientated society as it is associated with success and initiative that drives the successful. While the most dramatic combination remains the strong horse and strong rider that is mature with high energy, the Centaur.

The level of energy one possesses is a mixture of what you are born with (this is true for all Types) and how much energy you get from the residue of the horse rider battle. So you can have a high energy person that is un-integrated that may appear integrated (rising above all the usual daily problems) due to the natural high energy they are born with.

Then you have people who appear to have a high level of energy short term but don't really have it long term. This is because who we really are, and who we think we are, can be quite a different thing. We all wear masks from time to time that can mask our personality Type, even from ourselves.

Sometimes we do this for so long that we forget who we really are. We start to believe we are someone we are not. So one of the most important features of knowing yourself is how honest you are. And nobody is always Honest, except the Centaur. We all have agendas and egos that are inflamed to various degrees that distort our natural personality. The Centaur, being most mature, has the best chance of finding out whom he or she really is.

So remember when looking at other people, they might not be what Type you think they are. In divorce, this discrepancy sometimes is clearly manifested as the difference between the person you marry and the person you divorce. Generally there is a large gap. This gap could be due to the difference in Type and might be the reason for the divorce. The smaller the difference is, the more honest and mature the people are, the less acrimonious the divorce will be.

Also, the less gap there is, the better the chance of marital success. Immature Types tend to have the greatest gaps. The greater this gap is, and it can be positive or negative in nature, the greater the degree of un-integration. Meaning, a horse Or rider couple will be more likely to divorce and will have a greater gap (more painful divorce) than if two Level 1's divorce. Divorce results from the size of this gap. Thus the higher the integration of the horse rider systems that are involved, the less chance of divorce to begin with.

Prior to divorce, this gap can grow or shrink depending on the evolution of the integrations involved. People who evolve or integrate together will tend not to divorce as growth together builds bonds. So determining who you really are, and your mate as well, is critical as your Real level of integration determines things. And nothing shows oneself the TRUE level of their integration like divorce.

People are great at appearing something they are not. Some people find it exhausting trying to pretend to be a nice person but manage for a while and others can be nice with no energy expenditure at all. We all like to think we are experts at determining the difference when we see it but we have to look through our own filters to do it. The more well balanced your horse and rider, the more calm the ego, the truer the picture can become. And then there is less chance of waking up 10 years later with a person you don't recognize.

So that is the nature of the problem. What do we do in the meantime if we are an immature horse and/or rider waiting to evolve? Well, since you now have a better understanding/knowledge about what makes a horse and a rider tick, use this knowledge to address issues. First, and most important, try to integrate or evolve. Learn about the horse and rider. Calm the horse and rider using ideas from previous chapters.

If you are in a horse "OR" rider relationship the most important thing is to keep your horse and rider calm. Practice this until it becomes natural as this is the first step to integration. Then use the horse and rider integrated to grow, in order to change perspective. And if you can't integrate, and you are a horse in a rider relationship, remember what makes your partner tick and respond accordingly. Try to respond to the language he will understand. Talk and discuss things in a less emotional manner if dealing with types 1's and 2's. Address issues in a non-confrontational format. If angry, don't continue to address things as nothing ever got settled at this stage. If you are horse orientated (Type 4), consider that there are issues other than yours even if you think you know what is best for the other. Even if you think you supply lots of love, realize they may not want that quantity or value it the same. Any relationship that is too much of this or too little of that has a hard time surviving.

Remember riders don't like to talk about relationships but when forced to, will argue ad infinitum to justify their opinions. If you are a rider (Type 1) remember you know all the buttons to get your partners horse rearing, but it doesn't mean you have to push them. Develop your rider strengths to assist this. Use your discipline to help rather than to hinder. Stop poking your partner's horse and it will calm down and probably give you what you want.

It's interesting to try this approach and when it works you may actually learn to apply it to your own horse. Reverse the application. Naturally if these ideas are applied in balance with your partner they will spiral upward. The trick is to not let the balance get too far one way or the other. Remember the seesaw. The reason this doesn't always work is because you are artificially trying to balance an out of balance system. If your horse and rider are in balance, it will work, and even if out of balance the principle will work for a while but only temporarily. Even this can lead to healing if there is motivation to change. This is worth thinking about as it explains why a lot of relationships fail.

Lack of communication is the main reason often cited for why relationships fail. This is really a function of a lack of integration which leads to lack of communication as they end up speaking different languages. Things too far apart can't communicate. More precisely, lack of integration between the two horse rider systems gives rise to the gap widening till no more integration or communication is possible between the two horse riders systems.... And on the positive side of this, the more you are integrated the more communication and further integration is possible. Thus you can either help each sink or swim. This is very similar to the horse, rider and body in the Circle Figure.

Also, remember that horses have different coping mechanisms, decision making styles and quirky behaviors than riders. Riders need to recognize, respect and address this. Differences can be an asset or liability depending on your perspective. Horse and riders express everything differently. This can be O.K.

So one horse to another will define and express love differently than a rider, same thing with riders. When they mix you get apples and oranges at first, but when mature you get a Level 1 Integration or a delicious fruit salad. The Parts are still there but mixed together to form something else. You just have to make sure you agree on the proportions of apples to oranges. You need the right blend of knowledge and emotion. This takes wisdom in tandem with knowledge. It's like having the knowledge that a tomato is a fruit and not a vegetable but you don't put it in a fruit salad. Well I don't know about you but I'm getting hungry.

I think a note is appropriate here about how to go about picking a potential mate based on horse rider theory. When one is considering whether to get involved with a potential mate, what are the important things to look for? Well by now this should all sound somewhat familiar. The first and most important thing is, what level of integration have they achieved? Are they a horse Or rider? Are they a Level 1 Integration? A Level 2 Integration? A Centaur? The second question is, What Type are they? Type 1,2,3, or 4? The third question is, What level of maturity are they at?, as represented by their strengths and weaknesses.

So by now you have should an idea what all these should look like. But how do you tell how integrated someone is? I will say the more integrated you are, the better and more accurately you will be able to tell in another. A Centaur can spot another instantly, a Level 2 can also after very little time. A Level 1 has a bit more trouble. One way to help you is to see how "happy" they are. And remember I am using my definition of happy here. Do they operate near their limit? How do they answer the questions found in the first pages of this book? Do they have some checks from both lists? Are they mostly from one list?

I know people who married their first mate because they were captivated And fooled by the rider and his positives and the same people got married again to their second mate where they were captivated And fooled by the positives of the horse. The answer lies in the middle. And being able to discern what the middle is. And if that mate is really in the middle. And being in the middle yourself. The more integrated you are, the quicker you can jump into the dating pool and survive. And even if you aren't integrated this knowledge helps to discern reality.

We are all on this planet to discern reality. We have a bucket with us. When we experience something it can be considered to be either garbage or a diamond. We are supposed to pick up the diamonds and discard the garbage. Unfortunately, there are a lot of people walking around with buckets of garbage thinking they are succeeding. Centaurs have buckets of diamonds.

When I was on one of those internet dating sites, I noticed two of the most common things a woman was looking for in a man was, "Is he funny?" and, "Is he smart?" Notice how she was really asking, "Is he integrated?" (meaning funny=horsey And smart=rider). The very fact a person is looking for a smart And funny mate indicates that person is integrated and thus logically is seeking another integrated person. Can he/she also find both? Everybody loves and wants a Centaur! The Centaur is that elusive quarry possessing the ingenuity to boldly integrate education and entertainment to mesmerize people with its magical, innocent, passionate love of life and dazzle people with knowledge of arcane, mysterious, unknown forces that explain the universe. This is what we all seek, to help explain "it" to us so we can integrate, to become one with it all. Or just to allow us to live everyday of our lives and not just exist.

So that concludes an analysis of the development of horse and rider individually and in combination with another, and up to the Centaur level of development. What comes next? The Centaur continues to evolve as it fine tunes itself. It becomes more energy efficient. It matures, integrates more, and examines the universe with its integrated perspective and ample available energy. Keep in mind that as you integrate, evolve, grow through this process, the degree of available energy increases with each step. Thus with each level of integration there is more "happiness" as well as awareness.

The Centaur lives both inside and outside the box. It can honestly examine the nature of itself and the collective unit of all horse rider entities. The doorway to spirituality is now Really open. Now it is possible to touch the face of God. As we are one. God meaning unity.

CHAPTER SIX

There is no gift without a problem And
no problem without a gift.

So we have seen how the horse and rider have
their different perspectives, how this creates conflict,
how to calm them down, and how this allows a
broader perspective and further integration to occur.
How changing one's perspective allows for growth.
Then we saw how the horse and rider work in a
personal relationship, and now we will look at the
horse and rider as expressed at a cultural level.

Everything that is most important to us in our
culture consists of components that originate with the
horse And rider. This includes topics like music, art,
literature, politics, movies, religion, sports. etc.

Let's look at culture in general first. I spent a lot of
time on the islands surrounding Tahiti. The most
salient feature, that really impressed me the most,
was the native outlook on life (mostly Type 4's). They
don't really have a sense of time like we do. I
remember asking a desk clerk when the shuttle bus
arrived to take people to the main island. He
responded, "When it gets here". He wasn't being flip,
he just meant he was unconcerned about the future or
predicting it. He lived in the now, that was all that
was important. We in the West are obsessed about
time and being on time, controlling time. Things have
to occur when we say and when we want.

The Tahitians also have very laissez faire views on
most things. They don't look at ownership as we do in
the west. I was talking to a desk clerk about the high

grass around the resort. He said that somebody borrowed the mower and he didn't know when, or if, it would return. They tend to not attach ownership to things, even land. One guy I talked to said he found it odd how we can own land. He responded with, "Can you also own the wind and rain too".

They have a very relaxed structure about sex too. I asked him about it and he said if you wanted to have sex with a girl you just ask her. Usually they say yes he said. If you have ever seen or heard about the movie or movies titled something like, "Mutiny on the Bounty" then you have an idea how the Tahitians view things. Curious, in the movie, how the rigid Captain Bligh (Type 1) confronted the heathens of Tahiti (Type 4). Notice the stark contrast between Bligh (a staunch "civilized" rider) and the horsey Tahitians. We love it when horse meets rider (especially when it is strong rider meets strong horse) and this theme plays out in Hollywood all the time, probably unnoticed by most. We love it because we subconsciously like to see how others deal with this tension produced when horse and rider inter-react. We like to see the Hollywood horse do things we are reluctant to do. We like to see if maybe we could learn a thing or two about how we might deal with the tension inside ourselves when the two inter-react.

I could go on and on about similar features in Tahitian society but by now I think you get the drift that they are a horsey culture. Now some people dislike this. The first time I visited there, I was a little taken aback by the fact that there wasn't schedules for everything that I could depend on. That was the rider in me trained by our culture. But after a while I got used to it.

I might add it was a very short while before it seemed ok to me. It was like my first experience on a nude beach. The guy I talked to said most westerners get used to being naked much faster than they thought, usually just a few hours. This is because the thin veneer of rider civilization can be "stripped" clean in a surprisingly short time. What can be conditioned can be counter conditioned quickly if it is the horse's natural state. So, needless to say, I loved Tahiti once I got used to it. Some people don't like it, usually the riders because they miss the structure of western life. Some people prefer more predictability.

But the only thing that is changeless is change. I should also point out that in my conversations with Tahitians it became very apparent that a driving goal in their life was to go to Los Angeles. They always say the words with a star struck, glossy eyed look. The seesaw is ubiquitous.

Now if you go to Japan, there is a more structured culture (mostly Type 1's). They have some rigid social and economic conventions and expectations to succeed in the rider world are intense. They are into business taken seriously and by the rules. They also have the highest suicide rate of any country. There is more organized structure, and success is measured only in a rider way. This culture appeals more to the riders set of conventions.

If you look at different cultures around the globe it is interesting how each has a particular bent toward either horse or rider. And naturally there are type 2 and type 3 versions of this.

This same phenomenon plays out in the USA too. Think of the difference between a typical New Yorker and a typical person from California. It's curious that they live on the two extremes geographically as well as temperament. While cities are cosmopolitan (all Types) they none-the-less tend to display a particular "persona" that leans more toward horse or rider. Say, like the difference between New York and Las Vegas. Same thing occurs between Yankees and Southerners. Sometimes this out of balance conflict can even create wars.

Another example of this out of balance conflict is found in Hollywood movies that use the horse- rider motif, like Dr. Jekyl and Mr. Hyde (Type 1 and Type 4), or Avatar, where the rider style characters (Type 1) exploit and control the "hostile" alien planet, fighting the horsey aliens (Type 4) that are fighting to save their nature based culture. It is interesting that the public generally prefers Type 1 characters dealing with Type 4 characters rather than Type 2's interacting with Type 3's. There is naturally much more drama with the former.

Another example is any cowboy (Type 1) and Indians (Type 4) movie. Where the rider style cowboys characters are into taming the savage primitive, emotion filled, chaotic West in order to bring order and structure to the heathens. The whites are usually portrayed as the controllers; tighten their grip, dominators, rulers, superior to the earth based simple, natural, unstructured natives.

Another cinematic masterpiece of this idea is found in the old TV series MASH. The Hawkeye character was the horsey, unstructured, undisciplined doctor character while his bunk mate was Frank Burns (Type 1 Immature). Burns was disciplined, rigid, by the book, rules and order rule, no empathy or sympathy, support the establishment no matter what it did. The Burns character was a caricature of the rider, but the contrast between them gave rise to a lot of comedy because there is so much to work with when the horse and rider characters are extremes. The early Houlihan character (Type 1) was rider (desperately attempting to repress her natural horse) all the while trying to hide her horsey side until later in the show she changed (to Type 2) as the character matured, and came to terms with this.

Perhaps the most beautiful example of horse and rider in TV history is the old TV show "The Odd Couple". Felix (Type 1) and Oscar (Type 4) living together. Felix was the quintessential rider and Oscar was the quintessential horse. What a beautiful name for horse and rider, the odd couple. How appropriate. Felix was the quintessential horse with his prissy, logical, non-emotional approach to life. And Oscar was the quintessential horse, all sloppy, coarse, emotional approach to life. Yet they coexisted and integrated somehow and the differences made for entertaining TV as we loved to see how they did it.

In literature, Sherlock Holmes is the epitome of the rider character. Logic and rationality ruled him and defined him. Logic was the answer to solve all crimes. He didn't respond to, or acknowledge, anything other than rationality. Holmes was obsessed by the use of knowledge and rationality to solve crimes. Curiously, he was addicted to cocaine and playing the violin which he used to pacify his horse when it acted up beyond his means to control it. His partner, Dr. Watson was an educated responsible doctor who was more balanced and sympathetic and thus more blended with a broader perspective.

Music is another example of a popular facet of our culture that exemplifies horse and rider. The lyrics are for the rider and the melody is for the horse. One without the other doesn't have the broad based appeal that the mixture possesses. Musicians, being naturally horsey, generally create the melody first then fill in the rider lyrics later. They often use various mechanisms to remove the rider from the experience to allow the music to flow. There is a big difference in playing the notes and "making music". The difference is how involved the horse is and how not involved the rider is.

Musicians can create a song and then have to market it, so they need a rider because that process is the opposite of making music. This also shows how difficult it is for the two to integrate, though musicians have a special way of harmonizing horse and body. And sometimes when music is just right, the body also joins in and dancing results..

Sports is another example of the popularity of the mixture which also has the body joining in. Sports allow the horse to be expressed in a rider approved manner. The horse shows up in the aggressive tendencies that have an outlet on the field. The participants and the spectators share the power of the emotional release from supporting the team. The herd rallies around its members and various displays are a show of solidarity that cement the unifying principle. It is not a coincidence that sports teams are often named after animals or other natural symbols that the horse responds to. The social instinct and the aggressive instincts are satisfied. The rider enjoys the fact that there are rules that must be followed, and an order that defines the game. In a lot of human culture there are what we call "games" that are really very important and sometimes Darwinian in nature.

Take kids (Type 4) games for example. Hide and seek and tag. Hide and seek has rules that help define the "game" but in reality it has very serious consequences. The skill to successfully hide from a predator was very valuable a while back before our survival was more or less secured. To seek a prey was a valuable skill that had survival value. At this time in our development the horse was paramount. The game of tag develops similar skills. It is not amazing that kids all over the globe in all cultures play the exact same games, though they are called different names. The horse is ubiquitous through all cultures. It just manifests differently, religion does the same thing.

An interesting common denominator of the games we play is that they all have rider rules. Imagine any of these games without rules and their appeal wanes.

What you would then have is war. War is a uniquely human enterprise that shows what happens when the immature rider is allowed to be expressed without mature rider influence. War used to be mostly about winning at all costs, with very few rules bothered with, except the strongest rider wins, often because it also had the strongest horse on its side. It has evolved in recent times because the rider has decided to impose more rules, like the Geneva

Convention, which are somewhat adhered to by some cultures. People have come to see an uncontrolled rider (a dictator) as a distasteful beast. The civilized rider would rather there be rules so it can dominate the game and civilize it properly.

Some types of games do not have as strong an appeal across the social spectrum, like chess or jeopardy, for example which are mostly a rider type of game. The prototypical most enjoyable game always involves a healthy mix of chance and skill (horse and rider), usually well blended.

Though sometimes there are special games like lotteries that are pure luck or pure horse/body. But lotteries are for immature riders or poor mathematicians. Gambling also falls in this category. The body is susceptible to this game because it wants more. But the math generally determines the winner. A strong rider is required if the body is to be expressed without inflicting damage.

Addictions come in many flavors. Gambling starts with the body and it gets the horse/body on board usually to its peril. Horses/body can also get addicted to things like infatuation and things of the senses but also to money. The body can also get involved with addictions to drugs with the permission of a weak rider. A weak or low energy rider usually creates the recipe for future disaster. A strong, energetic rider permits indulgences to be amusing but without serious side effects. Similarly in diets, the strong rider fosters dietary success which overcome the urges of the horse and body.

However, with all these previously mentioned games, the horse often dictates who wins, by determining who uses their horse's power most efficiently. There is skill/knowledge of the game and there is emotional energy that combine to decide the superior balance of the two. Often in sports it is the most well balanced mixture of horse and rider that wins in the long run. In sports, if you get too high after a win, you will enjoy this but will probably lose the next game, too low after a loss and you will probably lose the next game. The balance is critical to success (Type 2 or 3).

The point is to use the rider to help determine this. But the rider must be accurate. The rider can mitigate things but he must have good judgment and good information to be useful. A rider with inaccurate knowledge is not helpful.

A mature horse and rider is wise. Wisdom can be defined as a mature horse and rider. The Centaur can understand and direct the horse component most efficiently and the Centaur can understand and direct the rider component most efficiently. The Centaur knows when to trust the horse's intuition and when to trust the rider's knowledge. It understands the true distinction between horse and rider.

Curiously enough, the whole distinction between horse and rider elements starts at birth. And most often, this is determined by birth order.

It is most interesting that horse or rider traits can be determined by birth order. First-borns are generally rider orientated (Type 1) and second-borns tend to be horse orientated (Type 4). Think about this in your own family. Notice if there are only two kids born, how they are polar opposites, not just a little different, but polar, 180 degrees different.

First-borns are known for being achievement oriented, structured, organized, analytical, good at math. Middle kids tend to be a blend of horse and rider and third-borns tend to be most horsey in nature. They are the musicians, artists, non-linear, non-structured type of people. First-borns bring out the rider in the parents and are often told what and how to do everything, while the later born are allowed more freedom to experience life more. Also I believe first-borns are more rider orientated and tense because moms with their first birth experience are more tense, and the kids pick up on this. Thus producing and enhancing this schism.

In politics there is a schism between Democrats (mostly Type 4) and Republicans (mostly Type 1). The Democrats are socially oriented, more inclusive and tolerant of all groups, more live and let live. The Republicans are more linear, black and white, individualistic, survival of the fittest, and more capitalistic.

In religion there is a component of horse and rider that is expressed culturally. There is a big difference between eastern and western religions. The eastern ones, Buddhism, Taoism, Confucianism are more horsey than the western versions. The eastern religions and philosophies emphasize holistic, inclusive, outside the box, approaches. The West is more rider based with more rigid, inside the box structure to their theologies and philosophies. Riders want to control the horse, using religious dogma to do it. "Thou shalt"...rules and dogma are used to attract the rider, while the horse wants the group identity. The rider uses this to exploit the horse. The church then exploits both horse and rider, suppressing both. A very similar process is found in the military (Type 1's quintessential)). See why?

It is time to discuss the notion of religion and spirituality here. And, yes, they can be radically different.

When I was growing up I came upon the subject of religion. Religion I came to see is spirituality put in a box. I was taught that being a Protestant was "right", thus all others were wrong. I then started thinking, how can one group be "right" and all the others "wrong"? The Protestants weren't the smartest of all peoples so why should they get it right and everybody else get it wrong? So why should everyone else have to go to hell for not believing correctly?

So I concluded that no one group could be right and thus everybody was wrong. So I became an agnostic, but after a while this didn't sit very well either. Then I had an epiphany. God is too all encompassing to fit into only one religion. So I concluded that they all got it right. All the major religions of the world are right. God is found in all of them. If you look at them at their roots, they have similar messages, all relating culturally to the local horse and rider expression.

So I came to believe that there is one over- arching entity that gets expressed in different ways depending on the cultural it is expressed in. It gets called different things depending on what part you are looking at.

It is a lot like the story of the three blind men and the elephant. One blind man touched the elephant's ear and concluded the elephant was thin and flexible.

Another touched the trunk and concluded the elephant was like a hose. Another touched the foot and concluded the elephant was like a tree. All three were right And wrong. A broader perspective allows for seeing reality clearer.

So, this over-arching entity gets called "God" in the west and Allah in the Middle East and Taoism in the East. It is like a tree with the roots in the earth branching out into branches with each leaf describing a different aspect of itself, sometimes called Methodists, Catholics, Buddhists, Muslims, etc. The farther one gets from the root the more mans influences carries it away from the essence. So we see that all is unified from the beginning then we get broken into component parts and spend the rest of our lives searching to go back to unity. Sound familiar?

When all of these ideas talked about in this book become incorporated into our young species on a broad basis, there will be a lot less killing and hatred and more understanding, patience and tolerance. Peace, love, and freedom will then become harmonized and coexist with knowledge, drive, and accomplishment to produce a Centaur race that will nourish our species and planet. Imagine what happens when everyone shares this view. It will happen...sigh.

So as a species we evolved from the lizard brain of our primitive ancestors to create a rider to assist and guide the horse, and now we are set to experience what it will be like when the two are compatibly integrated to produce a species of "Centaurs" who will influence all cultures to truly know themselves, truly know others, truly respect others and finally achieve our destiny. And what will happen after this occurs? ....We'll see. But just imagine what the future collective Centaur of our species says when it speaks!

A Centaur Speaks
A New and Exciting Way to Integrate Your Psyche

By Eric Barkemeyer

A CENTAUR SPEAKS: A New and Exciting Way to Integrate your Psyche - This book is an instruction manual about how to be highly successful in any area of your life. This is accomplished by exploring how to Integrate two of the most mysterious, miraculous and powerful components of the human psyche that are locked deep inside us all. I will take you on a fun and scary journey to integrate parts of your psyche that you have kept safely locked away. I will take you to magical places within yourself that you have never dared go to before, but have always suspected to exist. I will help you to unleash yourself and become a Centaur. Only the brave AND curious dare proceed, for courage AND curiosity are part of what I seek to Integrate, to create powers greater than each individually. Prepare to Expand your AND.

ABOUT THE AUTHOR

Eric Barkemeyer, former college professor of Astronomy, Physics and Geology, former stock market guru, former terminal cancer patient, former cowboy/dude ranch owner, former Millionaire, is now a humble novelist living a Simple life searching for the ultimate truth in the Universe.